The Griots' Cookbook

RARE AND WELL-DONE

By Alice McGill, Mary Carter Smith & Elmira Washington

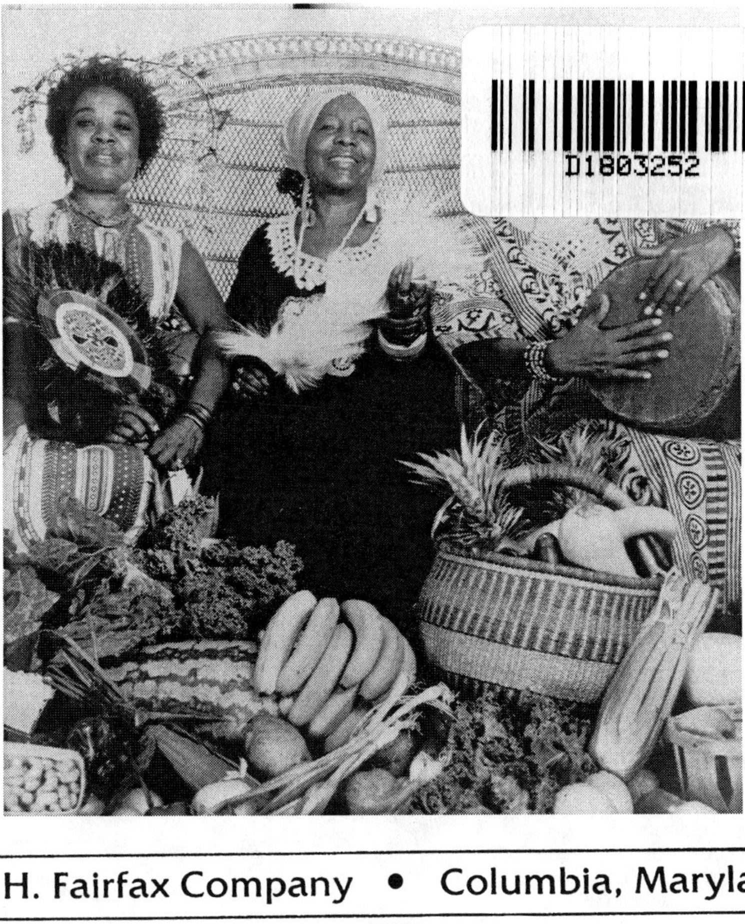

C.H. Fairfax Company • Columbia, Maryland

CHF

Copyright © 1985 by Alice McGill,
Mary Carter Smith, and Elmira Washington.

All rights reserved. No part of this book may be reproduced or transmitted in any form by any means, electronic or mechanical, including photocopying and recording, or by any information storage or retrieval system, without permission in writing from the publisher.

Published by C.H. Fairfax Company
Paul F. Evans, Publisher
Post Office Box 502
Columbia, Maryland 21045
(301) 730-2397

ISBN 0-935132-05-8
Manufactured in the United States of America
Photo Credits: Bruce Smallwood
John Kraft - Graphics

Library of Congress Card Number 85-82113
Published, December, 1985
Second Printing, March, 1986

Dedicated to future generations of cooks and storytellers.

Acknowledgements

First, we give honor to God, our Creator and Jesus, our Lord, for inspiring us to create this book and strengthening us as we bring it to fruition.

Our thanks to Super Pride Markets, Inc. for providing the food used in the cover photograph.

Special thanks to our husbands, Purnell Washington and Marion McGill, who perservered through the planning, writing, editing and the never-ending meetings.

We want to acknowledge the staff and volunteers at Morgan State University's radio station, WEAA-88.6 FM, for their help in producing "Griot for the Young and Young-at-Heart."

Our final and most special gratitude is humbly extended to all of you good cooks who so graciously tendered us your treasured recipes. Without you there could be no "rare and well done!"

. . . Especially for you –
You who are young
and
you who are young at heart.

– Mary Carter Smith

From "Griot for the Young and Young at Heart,"
WEAA-88.9 FM

Contents

List of Illustrations/Recipe Contributors XV
Foreword .... Mary Carter Smith XVII
Introduction .... Lillie G. Patterson XIX
                                                                                                                 Page

THE GRIOTS 1
    Autobiographical Sketches:
        Alice McGill 5
        Mary Carter Smith 9
        Elmira M. Washington 13

KITCHENCRAFT 17
    Checklist for Beginning Cooks   Hints
    Equivalency Chart   Nutrition Tips
    Equivalents   Party Planning
    Food Facts and Fancies

THE RECIPES 25
    Recipe for Elephant Stew 26
    BITS n' PIECES 27
        Banana Salad   Macaroni and Cheese
        Barbecue Sauce #1   Milk and Bread
        Barbecue Sauce #2   Mix
        Bum Bye   Rose Sachet
        Carrot Salad Delight   Sherried Custard Sauce
        Cucumber Dip   Stuffing Outside of the Turkey
        Dill Dressing   Especially For Children
        Incredible Pie Crust   Potato Press
        Jo's Spaghetti   Sculpture with Dough
        Kwanza Salad   Summer Solar Bowl
        Leftover Chili   Toasted Pumpkin Seeds
        Low Calorie Fruit Salad

    BREADS 49
        Fancy Cornbread   Quick Zucchini Bread
        Pumpkin Bread   Refrigerator Rolls

    EGGS 55
        Confetti Omelette   Potato Chip Omelette
        Deviled Eggs   Salmon Souffle

    MEATS/FISH/POULTRY 61
        African Chicken   June's Shrimp Fried Rice
        Apricot Chicken   June's and Pie's Pig Feet and Rice
        Barbecued Chicken & Spareribs   Meat Loaf
        Bernardo Crab   Mountain Oysters
        Brule Jol (West Indian Codfish)   Neck Bones and Rice
        Buttered Shrimp   Nigerian Stew
        Chicken and Cabbage   Oyster Stew
        Chicken Noodle Bake   Rice with Chicken
        Chicken Pie   Roast Beef
        Chicken Pot Pie   Roast Chicken (Old Fashioned)
        Cousin George's Chicken   Roast Goose/Directions for
        Curried Stove Top Chicken   Trussing Poultry
        Fish and Okra   Roast Possum with Sweet Potatoes
        Fried Chitterlings   Shrimp Meat Sauce
        Grilled Shrimp Catonsville   Souse
        Heart Chop Suey   Southern Fried Chicken
        Imperial Crab Topping   Steak and Rice
        Juicy Hamburgers   Stewed Chicken and Dumplings

Contents

SWEETS 101
    Alabama Coconut Pound Cake
    Ambrosia
    Autumn Woodlawn Cake
    Banana Pudding
    Bitsy's Light Fruit Cake
    Black Raspberry Cobbler
    Cheese Cake
    Cold Oven Pound Cake
    Coconut Pie
    Cream Puffs/Cream Filling
    Five Flavor Pound Cake
    Fresh Peach Pie
    Fresh Plum Pie
    Fried Orange Delite
    Friendship Cake
    Grandmom's Sweet Potato Cake
    Harvest Cake
    Hot Milk Cake
    Lemon Dainty
    Lemon Meringue Pie
    Lemon Stack Pie
    Mama's Tea Cakes
    Miss Marie's Sweet Potato Pie
    Old Fashioned Carrot Cake
    Philly Pound Cake
    Plain Cake
    Quick Fudge Brownies
    7UP Pound Cake
    Southern Apple Cobbler
    Sweet Potato Pie
    Sweet Potato Pudding #1
    Sweet Potato Pudding #2
    Trifle
    Unbelievable Peanut Butter Cookies
    Vanilla Ice Cream
    Watergate Salad
    Wonderful German Apple Cake

VEGETABLES 143
    Akara
    Baked Beans
    Baked Potatoes in Blankets
    Beans: White, Boiled, Vegetarian
    Boiled Carrots
    Candied Sweets
    Coleslaw with Tomatoes
    Corn Pudding
    Crisp Stringbeans
    Feijoada (Black Beans)
    Fried Green Tomatoes
    Fried Okra, Corn and Tomatoes
    Greens
    Greens in Chicken Broth
    Hoppin' John
    Hot Vegetable Salad for One
    Macaroni Salad
    Marinated Cucumbers
    Marinated Tomatoes
    Mushrooms and Scallions
    Mushrooms in Cheese Sauce
    Okra Stew
    Poke Salad
    Potato Salad
    Ratatouille with Mushrooms
    Sauerkraut
    7 Layer Salad
    Stringbeans, Carrots and Onions
    Stuffed Baked Potatoes
    Stuffed Cabbage Rolls
    Vegetable Medley
    Yellow Squash Souffle

THE STORIES 177
    The Last Shot .... Alice McGill 179
    Notes on Cindy Ellie 184
    Cindy Ellie...................... Mary Carter Smith...................... 185
    The Doberman's Dilemma .... Elmira M. Washington 191

STORYTELLING 197
    Storytelling .... Linda Goss 198
    How I Make A Story A Part Of Myself .... Mary Carter Smith........... 199
    Tidbits for Telling Stories .... Mary Carter Smith 200
    Pitfalls 201

List of Illustrations

Kitchencraft 17
Bits n' Pieces 27
Breads 49
Eggs 55
Meats/Fish/Poultry 61
Sweets 101
Araber 142
Vegetables 143

Recipe Contributors

Rachel K. Baumgartner
Mozella Blackwell
Frances Branch
Therese Chambers
Juanita Clark
Sallie Lou Coleman
Rita Cox
Gloria Davis
Verna Day
Louis Denson
Lillian Fleet
Marie Foster
Louise Gambrill
A. Katherine Gross
Irene Holland
Henrietta Holliman
Mable Hubbard
Marie Humphrey
Joann Kelly
Earl Kidwell
Susie Knight
Joan Kraft
Virgie Lawson

Charlotte Little
Willie N. MacAdory
Alice McGill
Fred McLean
Harriett McLean
Priscilla L. Marshall
Freda Mason
Vernon H. Mason, Jr.
Thelma B. Mason
William Mumby, Sr.
Venezuela Newborn
Mary D. Nowden
Nowden Family
Mary Olandu
Elizabeth M. Oliver
Maisha E. Parker
Emmanuel Pennick
Nancy Peverley
Mayner Pope
Lila Powell
Linda Richardson
Joyce Robertson
Dorothy Ross

Gwendolyn N. Samuels
Odessa M. Segers
Vanessa M. Simms
Mary Carter Smith
William Spencer
George Stevenson
Joan Stevenson
Lola Taylor
Mary Taylor
Thomas Taylor
Delores Terry
Margaret C. Turner
Constance Washington
Elmira M. Washington
Joi L. Washington
June Washington
Marjorie D. Washington
Purnell (Pie) Washington
Doris Waters
Margaret Williams
DeWildera Willoughby
S. Josephine Wing-Shelton
Ruth Ann Zeller

Foreword

Like Topsy, this book "jus' growed." Since Morgan State University's WEAA-FM went on the air eight years ago, I have been blessed to produce and present the program, *"GRIOT FOR THE YOUNG AND YOUNG AT HEART."* One of my aims is to share what I have experienced with younger people of talent, so that the griot tradition will pass on. Several griots-in-training have worked with me and gone into other fields. For the past two years, Alice McGill and Elmira Washington have worked with me. They have brought diversity and vitality to the program.

The idea of producing a cookbook began with Elmira Washington. We wanted to help the station's fund-raising. Alice and I agreed that the idea was a good one. We are giving copies of the book as gifts to the first twenty-five donors of at least $100.00. Since the three of us are writers as well as storytellers, we are including some of our writings as part of the book.

Recipes come from many sources. Some are original. Some are favorites that deserve to be shared. Some of mine I have picked up in my travels. Always the three of us work as a team. I thank Alice and Elmira for their dependability and willingness to share their gifts. All of us are volunteers.

We hope you enjoy reading and using the book half as much as we enjoyed creating it.

We are grateful for the expertise and encouragement of our editor and publisher, Paul Evans.

Mary Carter Smith

Introduction

Food is life. **Cooking**, the preparation of food, is a creative art that brings about transformation in appearance, flavor, texture, and taste. **Storytelling** is an art, an art that is as old as language. When a single volume contains examples of the art of cooking and also examples of storytelling, the result is as entertaining as it is useful.

The Griots' Cookbook displays the creativity and talent of three griots. Mary Carter Smith is known internationally as a griot. She has travelled across the United States, displaying her artistry, and in the meantime collecting stories and folk materials to share with children and adults. This dedicated artist works with a mission to pass along her skills to other storytellers.

Two of the griots-in-training, Alice McGill and Elmira Washington, have teamed with their mentor to produce a unique guide for anyone who enjoys experimenting with the art of food preparation. Some of the recipes are family favorites, passed along as treasured works of art. Other recipes are original, perfected in much the same way as these artists perfect their storytelling – creating, revising, sharing until a perfect form emerges that evokes the exclamation, "That is good!"

Among the most interesting recipes are those adapted from friends in African countries. Coupled with these are tried-and-true dishes borrowed from friends of the griots who live in Baltimore and elsewhere. The major food groups are included as well as the various forms of food preparation.

There is more. Biographical sketches introduce us to the griots and the fascinating lives they lead. Coupled with these are original stories, poems and humorous anecdotes.

The pages contain a potpourri of useful tips for kitchen artists of all ages. For example, a checklist for beginning cooks will be useful for anyone operating in a kitchen.

Have you tried growing herbs? Can you make **good** homemade ice cream? Do you have a "Happy Home Recipe"?

The answers are all here in this fascinating volume. You will chuckle while you cook, and long after the food is eaten. You may even decide to become a griot, as well as a cook.

The Griots' Cookbook is a one-of-a-kind treasure, combining the art of cooking and the art of storytelling.

Lillie Patterson

The Griots

Alice McGill

Alice McGill

Alice McGill

At this writing I am a long way from my home in Harford County, Maryland and a long way from my birthplace in Scotland Neck, North Carolina. As the old folks used to say, "There's been a heap said and done" on my way from Scotland Neck to where I am now in Artpark.

Artpark is a center for cultural arts, sponsored by New York State. I am the resident storyteller for one week. The storytelling place is situated in a small clearing in a big wood. When the wind rustles through the leaves, I can see the brightly-colored trams as they stop at the foot of the hill. Soon people will walk up the hill to the storytelling place. At the end of the hour's session many will remain seated on the logs to ask questions about my background. We will swap tales and anecdotes. I feel at home in this small clearing in the woods. Even the rich black dirt reminds me of the fertile farmland of my childhood.

I was born to the late Norman S. and Ella G. Pope in a small house in a small clearing in a wood. My mother gave birth to ten children in that three-room house. Only eight children survived to adulthood. I was "smack-dab in the middle," and I was the middle girl.

My earliest memory of myself was that of pestering my father on the night of my fourth birthday. I had been told that I could not possibly become four-years old until eleven o'clock p.m. which was the moment of my birth.

Although we went to bed with the chickens during the winter, (I was born in February), I persisted in nudging him every half hour or so to ask, "Am I four, yet?" He finally said, "You four years old now. Go back to sleep." Needless to say, I slept soundly for the rest of the night.

I attended a three-room country school that housed grades from one through eight. I was 12 years old before I traveled more than 10 miles away from home.

I remember the day we had the house wired for electricity. I remember my first store-bought dress. I remember picking cotton, shaking peanuts, and pulling corn.

With today's modern farming techniques, there's no wonder that my own children asked me, "Did they have pencil sharpeners when you were little?"

I was born just before WWII and times have changed in leaps and bounds ever since. I attended Brawley High School in Scotland Neck and during my 12th year, I was awarded a $500 scholarship due to my speaking and acting abilities.

Strangely enough, the scholarship was from a teacher's college, Elizabeth City State Teacher's College, which is now Elizabeth City State University. I grew to know that good teachers are good actors.

While working in Baltimore during the summer to earn money for college, I met my husband and best friend, Marion McGill. We have two daughters, Paulette and Gwendolyn. While helping to raise our "little" family, I taught school over 20 years and then decided to pursue a career in acting, modeling, and storytelling. Of the three job descriptions, storytelling is more natural as everyone has a story to tell.

I have been out of the classroom almost two years now. I feel that I have experienced the best of both worlds – the world of the regular job holder and the world of the freelancer.

Through storytelling I met Mary Carter Smith and Elmira Washington, who are two of the most competent storytellers I know.

My acting performances have led me to the National Theatre in Washington D.C., The Smithsonian Institution, bit parts in major motion pictures, and television commercials, however, storytelling remains the bottom line because storytelling is the base of what I am about.

Alice McGill

Mary Carter Smith

Mary Carter Smith

Mary Carter Smith

I was born in Birmingham, Alabama. My mother died when I was four. I lived briefly, in Lynch, Kentucky. I moved with grandmother, Mary Days Nowden, to Youngstown, Ohio to join my uncle, Anderson Nowden.

During summers of my childhood, I visited my three aunts in many small mining communities of West Virginia. My grandmother and I lived a short while in Evertsville, West Virginia with an aunt.

Later my grandmother and I moved back to Birmingham. My grandmother became ill and my aunt, Willie Nowden McAdory, took us to Edwight, West Virginia to live with her and her husband. There my dear grandmother died in May, 1932. Our family moved to Ida May, West Virginia. My aunt, known as Aunt Booby, lost her sight. We moved to Baltimore so Aunt Booby could be treated at Johns Hopkins Hospital. She regained her sight.

Mary Rogers Coleman was my maiden name. I was graduated from Douglass High School and Coppin Teachers' College. Louise Monroe and I were the first blacks allowed to work as typists at Social Security's Candler Building where I worked at night during my last year at Coppin.

I enjoyed working as an elementary teacher and librarian in the Baltimore City Public Schools. By choice I worked only in the inner city. Securing futher degrees did not interest me. I secured many credits in oral narration, theater, literature, etc. in several institutions including New York University, Catholic University of America, Temple Buell University, Johns Hopkins University, Rutgers University, and the University of Maryland.

Sedonia Merritt and I founded Big Sisters-Little Sisters, Inc. It is now part of Big Brothers-Big Sisters of Central Maryland. I am also a founding member of the Big Sisters International that became part of Big Brothers-Big Sisters of America.

I was one of the first members of the Arena Players, Inc. founded by Samuel Wilson.

I retired from the city schools to accept a job as hostess of "Black Is" with the Maryland Corporation for Public Broadcasting. I made the first of seven trips to Mother Africa in 1970.

I felt God's call to be His messenger of peace, with justice and traveled throughout the United States, four of the Caribbean Islands, parts of England and France as a griot. Most of my appearances have been in the city schools of Baltimore. The Smithsonian Institution, and the Kennedy Center are among many places where I have made appearances as a professional griot.

In 1983, Linda Goss of Philadelphia and I founded the National Festival of Black Storytelling. The first festival was in Baltimore in November, 1983. At that time Mayor William Donald Schaefer proclaimed me as "Official Griot of Baltimore."

Since I am interested in the community, I have worked with many groups such as the Citizens' Coalition for Urban Survival, the Baltimore Rescue Mission, etc. I am grateful to have been honored by many organizations.

Some of the many people and groups who encouraged and helped were Huber Memorial Church of Christ, the Kittamanundi Community, Langston Hughes, Alex Haley, James Rouse, Willnetta and Clearman Sutton and E. Lee Lassiter.

In 1946, I married Ulysses J. Carter. Our son, Ricardo Rogers Carter, was born February 17, 1948. In 1950, we were divorced. I married Elias Raymond Smith in July, 1960. He died in 1962.

I have authored three books: *Town Child, Vibes,* and *Heart ot Heart.*

I have also produced a record, a cassette tape, and two posters. For the past eight years, I have produced and presented an hourly program, "Griot for the Young and Young at Heart," at WEAA-FM at Morgan State University.

Since my son, Ricardo, was killed in January, 1978, I have rededicated my life to sharing Christ's message of love and the beauty of the "Black Experience."

These words I would leave with you: *"By this shall all men know that ye are my disciples, if ye have love one to another."* John 13:35

Mary Carter Smith

Elmira M. Washington

Elmira M. Washington

Elmira M. Washington

I am Sunday's child. The Easter celebration ran into the middle of April that year, and my journey from womb to world happened on Palm Sunday. Mama tells a special story about my birth.

Around 6:30 a.m. that Palm Sunday, my father, Vernon H. Mason, Sr., hailed a taxi on North Avenue near McCulloh Street where they lived. The cab driver took one look at Mama, as Daddy was helping her into his vehicle, and decided to make tracks. Mama declares the man broke every speed law on the books. He covered the distance to Johns Hopkins Hospital fast enough to set a new speed record. Mama was too busy to be scared. Between labor pains and keeping Daddy calm, she didn't have any attention left.

The cabbie succeeded in his quest. I was not born until Mama was wheeled into the hospital. Then, right under the statue of Jesus, Thelma Boyer Mason, was delivered of her first-born child.

How's that for an auspicious beginning? Naturally, I'd be bound to feel some fondness for that old rhyme that begins, "Sundays child is full of grace."

A great many Sundays have come and gone since then. I've used some of them well and some less than well. I've learned that the old rhyme is pure romance. That was one of my minor learnings.

Fortunately, the days that followed my first Palm Sunday have been crowded with goodness, spice and some major learnings. Of course, there have been times of illness, sorrow or dejection; even some failures. Still, the scales have been heavily weighted on the success side. I've been blessed with years of loving support.

My immediate family is small. I have one sibling, my brother, Hayward. Mama and Daddy loved us and gave us their full attention when we were youngsters.

Before I started school, Daddy taught me the alphabet and counting from 1 to 100. I guess he taught me to read - I can't recall **not** being able to read. I do remember that Daddy taught me to write and read all of the family members' names, my address and the name of the city. I thought BALTIMORE was such a pretty word.

My writing skills caused me problems as a first grader at Gilmor Elementary School. My teacher was appalled when she discovered that I had been taught and was only able to write in cursive. Daddy was pretty upset when I informed him that I was not allowed to write, only print, in first grade. He and the teacher finally agreed on a truce. I was allowed to "write" only until I mastered printing (which I never did until I attended Coppin). That was just a prelude to all the major teaching that helped mold me.

Mama taught me EVERYTHING. My little brother taught me all about filial devotion. My Aunt Sadie taught me to enjoy all kinds of good eating (she and I shared thick dark slices of raisin bread along with creamy vanilla ice cream and steaming cups of strong, black Chinese tea).

My Godmother, Aunt Blanche, showed me how to be generous and thoughtful of others, by setting a lovely example. My grandfathers, Pa and Papa, taught me to respect my elders by their wit, patience and manly charms. My cousin, Etta, taught me to crochet in order to distract me while my aunt, Nannie, was ill. Nannie, on her death-bed, taught me to face reality and the value of truth. My cousins on both sides taught me graphically, as peers are wont to do. All of my growing-up years were filled with positive contributions to my major learnings by relatives.

The best of the major learnings, was reading, which is the mainstay of my life. If ever I am blinded, I shall learn Braille immediately. I cannot imagine life without books. Reading is my escape; I can be anyone, go everywhere, do anything at anytime in the past, the present or the future. Reading teaches me, entertains me, informs me, enlarges my world, keeps me humble and satisfies my curiosity.

When I was a pupil in the three levels of schools that public education in Baltimore provided, I enjoyed myself, due in large part, to my love affairs with books. Despite a few times that I'm glad to have survived, I liked being a student. My parents' marriage faltered and dissolved, but Mama kept right on boosting my brother and me. Education was what she preached.

I followed her advice. I conquered Robert Brown Elliot Elementary School, Booker T. Washington Junior High School, and Frederick Douglass Senior High School, but Mama wasn't finished boosting yet. She insisted that I continue my education, she said I didn't "know enough yet." That's why I became a teacher. Mama told me to enroll at Coppin in February, right after being graduated from High School. When I finally did enroll, it was August and I'd made friends with some hard facts. Mama did not have money to send me elsewhere for more major learning. So off to Coppin I went.

Baltimore's educational system trained its black elementary teachers at Coppin Teachers' College on Mount Street. The third floor of Coppin Elementary School was the whole "college" in those days. I dubbed it "six rooms and two baths." We attended without charges (monetary) and were expected to take jobs in the Baltimore Public Schools for a minimum of two years upon successful completion of the four-year program.

They were the hardest, most emotion-laden years of my life, but I made it through. I took the required test, passed, and was given my first assignment as a classroom teacher. Mama was elated. I was terrified.

My teaching career tottered off on an unsteady footing but it did stabilize. I worked at it until I became a good, effective teacher because I loved working with the children, and I wanted to do my best with them. Thirteen years later I switched from the classroom setting to the school library. The next ten years were some of the happiest and most productive ones of my teaching career. I was surrounded by the two things I most cherished: books and children. During those years I put down roots and began to stretch myself professionally.

While I was a librarian, I began to appreciate storytelling as an enriching tool as well as a mode of entertaining others. I enjoyed it. There is nothing to equal the feeling you have when your audience, especially children, gives you their full attention.

My storytelling was appreciably enhanced by a sabbatical year of study at the University of Maryland. I earned my Master of Library Science degree that year. Most importantly, I acquired a treasure trove of knowledge (and honed my skills) to take back to my position as a teacher-librarian in a Baltimore elementary school. Those happy times went forward for another four years. During the following school year, I changed positions again. This time I switched back towards the classroom when I accepted a senior teacher position.

I was assigned to work at the same school. The children expected me to go on telling stories as I had in the library. That was impossible, but I made special efforts to share with them as often as I could. Halloween became an eventful day for the children and for me. They demanded their favorite spooky stories and poems; I happily acceded to their wishes. A couple of those stories are now part of my storytelling repertoire.

During my thirty-year teaching career, I gained a handsome husband, Purnell Washington, a beautiful daughter, Joi Lizette, and learned some hard lessons. I changed from a girl into a woman.

In retrospect, I prefer childhood. Its innocence and capacity for incredulity are far superior to the arrogance and mere capabilities of adulthood. That is not cynicism, just understanding on my part. I realize the clear differences between childhood and adulthood, but I prefer childhood. Perhaps my major teachings and learnings are what attract me; my childhood memories still succor me.

Now, during these latter days of my life, I am grateful and fortunate to be fulfilled. My friends, Mary Carter Smith and Alice McGill, keep contributing to my major learnings. It's a wonderful experience. They consistently boost me as I perform or write stories and poetry. Could I ask for more skilled advocates than they? Positively not! One is a master storyteller and folklorist. The other is a superb actress and yarn spinner. Both are gracious enough to share their knowledge and both are skillful enough to teach me. I love being their pupil; having them as mentors, and mostly, I adore having them as my sisters.

Let me end by telling you how I became such a ham. My brother ingeniously convinced us that he was illiterate. On Sundays, I was expected to read the entire comic section to him. Mama insisted! I loathed the chore at first, but it turned into a bonus for me.

Sometimes I would forget and go sailing through half a strip, reading swiftly and silently. Hayward would yell in indignation, "Ma, she's reading to herself again!" Then I'd have to reread orally all the parts I'd already covered. I began to ham up my readings, changing voices and personalities from strip to strip. What a great audience my little brother made. He rewarded my creative readings with gales of laughter. After those sessions of oral reading, I was almost an expert in using expression to enhance the printed word. I didn't know it then, but I was just one step from storytelling. So I owe my "little" brother untold thanks for indulging his laziness. He wasn't illiterate at all, just my first and most appreciative audience.

Today, my family is fully extended by the addition of two sets of Washingtons (with assorted relatives by marriage). My husband's large family contributes almost daily to my education and our nurturing. My brother's lovely wife has a large, friendly family that also brings richness into our lives.

Within the circle of love and caring formed by family, friends and my two sisters, I know gratitude and peace. Now that's a marvelous and fertile field for major learning to continue indefinitely. I'm looking forward to it.

Elmira M. Washington

Kitchencraft

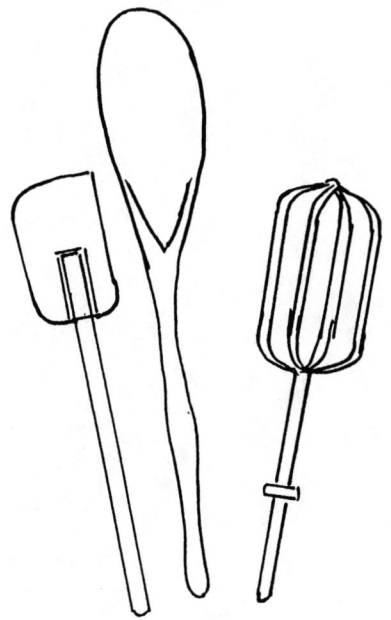

Checklist For Beginning Cooks

_____ Always read the entire recipe **Before** you are ready to use it.
_____ Assemble **All** ingredients in the kitchen when you are ready to cook.
_____ Check to see if you understand the cooking and preparation terms used in the recipe.
_____ Measure portions **Exactly**, using the proper utensils.
_____ **Always** hold measuring spoons away from the mixing bowl when pouring seasonings into them. You avoid mistakes and waste.
_____ Put everything you used back where it belongs during clean-up.
_____ Clean up as you cook; this saves a horrible job afterward.
_____ Write down and save any changes, additions (or deletions) you make in the recipes. Incidentally, if you concoct a new recipe, be sure to record the ingredients (in the order that you used them.)
_____ Be brave and **Taste** the food when it is done (if possible). Season according to your taste if necessary.
_____ Set an attractive table for all the good food you cook.

Equivalency Chart

When the recipe calls for:	You start with:
5½ cup cooked fine noodles	8 oz. pkg. fine noodles
4 cups sliced raw potatoes	4 med. size potatoes
2½ cup sliced carrots	1 lb. raw carrots
4 cups shredded cabbage	1 small cabbage
1 tsp. grated lemon rind	1 medium lemon
2 tbsp. lemon juice	1 medium lemon
4 tsp. grated orange rind	1 medium orange
4 cups sliced apples	4 medium apples
2 cups shredded swiss or cheddar cheese	8 oz. piece of swiss or cheddar cheese
1 cup bread crumbs	2 slices of bread
1 cup egg whites	6-7 large eggs
1 cup egg yokes	11-12 large eggs
4 cups chopped walnuts or pecans	1 lb. shelled walnuts or pecans

Equivalents

3 teaspoons - 1 tablespoon
4 tablespoons - ¼ cup
5⅓ tablespoons - ⅓ cup
8 tablespoons - ½ cup
10⅔ tablespoons - ⅔ cup
12 tablespoons - ¾ cup
16 tablespoons - 1 cup
½ cup - 1 gill
2 cups - 1 pint

4 cups - 1 quart
4 quarts - 1 gallon
8 quarts - 1 peck
4 pecks - 1 bushel
16 ounces - 1 pound
32 ounces - 1 quart
8 ounce liquid - 1 cup
1 ounce liquid - 2 tablespoons

(For liquid and dry measurements, use standard measuring cups and spoons. All measurements are level)

1. 1 square (1 ounce chocolate - 3-4 tablespoons cocoa plus ½ teaspoon fat.)
2. Sweet milk and baking powder, for baking-Equal amount of sour milk plus ½ teaspoon soda per cup. (each half-teaspoon soda with 1 cup sour milk takes place of 2 teaspoons baking powder and 1 cup sweet milk.)
3. 1 cup sour milk for baking - 1 cup sweet milk with one of the following: 1 tablespoon vinegar or 1 tablespoon lemon juice, or 1¾ teaspoons cream of tartar.
4. 1 cup skimmed milk - 4 tablespoons nonfat dry milk plus 1 cup water.
5. 1 cup cake flour for baking - ⅞ cup all-purpose flour.

Food Facts and Fancies

A few radishes left in the refrigerator? Chop them fine and add them to a sandwich filling of salmon, tuna or hard-cooked eggs.

Cut a slice from tops of small tomatoes and scoop out about ½ inch of the tomato pulp to form slight indentations. Fill indentations with minced onions and dot with butter, then sprinkle with paprika. Bake 325° for about 20 minutes.

To make juiciest hamburgers, add ⅓ cup applesauce for each pound of meat. Add other seasonings (as desired), shape and cook meat as usual.

Hints

To prevent fat from spattering when you are frying, sprinkle salt in the skillet before you add any fat or food.

A little butter or margarine added to spaghetti, macaroni or rice while cooking will prevent boiling over.

Cooked green vegetables stay bright green if cooked uncovered. Do not overcook.

To clear cloudy tea, add a little boiling water and stir.

To prevent flour from lumping, add a little salt before mixing with water or milk.

Nutrition Tips

Six helpful facts:
1. Overcooking hurts your food. Try broiling, steaming or using a pressure cooker; vitamins will be better preserved.
2. Don't peel turnips, potatoes, carrots, etc. Use a scrub brush to clean them; rinse before cooking. Peels are nutritious.
3. Add salt to food only after cooking, if at all. Salt causes nutrients to be lost during cooking.
4. Save celery leaves, outer cabbage leaves, and other vegetable scraps for soup stock. They are full of vitamins.
5. Use frozen food within 3-10 months. Vitamins are lost during over-long storage.
6. Make your snacking more nutritious. Eat dried fruits or fresh fruits; popcorn and peanuts are also good substitutes for "junk food".

Party Planning

Get a pencil and paper ready; make the following lists:
1. Guests
2. Foods
3. Supplies
4. Music
5. Beverages
6. Menu
7. Decorations
8. Furniture, or lack of, if you're making space
9. Shopping necessary
10. Housework
11. Closet space (in winter)
12. Alerting neighbors
13. Time
14. Clean-up

The Recipes

Recipe For Elephant Stew

Ingredients:
1 medium elephant, diced
Dash of salt and pepper
1 onion
1 package of elbow macaroni
2 rabbits

Directions:

After the 60 days that it takes to dice the elephant, put in a 5 ton casserole.
Add salt, pepper, onion and simmer gently for 6 weeks.
During the last seven minutes, add the macaroni. This serves 3,462 guests.
If the guests bring guests, add the rabbits, but only if absolutely necessary, because most people don't like to find hare in their stew.

Bits n' Pieces

Snowballs

When it's hot I go to Miss Rosie's house.
She has a table right outside
That's where you buy your cool snowballs
They are Miss Rosie's pride
Cherry, lemon, grape, and orange
The bottles are sitting around
She pours the sweet flavor over the ice
And your tongue sends the coolness down
     Mary Carter Smith
     ©1976

Hard times make a monkey eat red pepper.

The man who is not hungry says the coconut has a hard shell.

When the ape cannot reach the ripe banana with his hand, he says it is sour.

African Proverbs

Banana Salad

5 medium, firm bananas
1 lemon, juice and pulp
2 slim cucumbers
¼ teaspoon salt
6 stalks green onions
½ teaspoon sugar
1½ tablespoon mayonnaise

Directions
Peel and slice bananas into fairly thick slices. Place in bowl. Add pulp of lemon and enough lemon juice to coat slices. This helps bananas keep their color. Peel and slice cucumbers into thin slices. Place them in another bowl, add salt and toss. Combine bananas, cucumbers, sliced onions, sugar and mayonnaise. Toss lightly and serve.

Mary Carter Smith

The mother had been instructing Junior about proper pronunciation of words. The family was eating hot cakes and molasses for breakfast. Junior asked, "Ma, can I please have some more 'lasses?" "Junior, I told you to say molasses." Junior answered, "How can I have mo' lasses when I ain't had some lasses?"

Barbecue Sauce #1

1 fresh lemon
1 cup water
1 cup sugar (brown or white or you may
    substitute syrup or honey)
    salt, black pepper, red pepper or sauce, dry mustard,
    powdered ginger, catsup, Worcestershire sauce,
    vinegar, garlic salt or powder to taste.
2 onions, chopped

Directions
Wash and cut lemon into eighths. Place them with water and sugar into pot and boil until thick. Then add other ingredients to taste. For example, only a small jar of catsup is needed, then add enough vinegar to give sweet-sour taste and add other ingredients unitl sauce tastes "right." Put cooked meat such as chicken, ribs, or lamb necks into barbecue sauce and simmer on top of stove until meat is very tender. Stir often to keep sauce from sticking.

                                                              Nowden Family

Barbecue Sauce #2

1 can crushed tomatoes
1 can tomato sauce
2-4 light brown onions, chopped
1 clove of garlic, chopped
1 bay leaf
2 tablespoons oil (your choice)
Lemon juice (from the bottle)
Mustard, ginger, chili powder, pepper,
celery salt, brown sugar,
Worcestershire sauce
Apple jelly

Directions
   Begin by mixing the tomatoes and the tomato sauce. Then add all other ingredients as listed. Where no specific measurement is given, you must follow the cook's directions:
   "Just keep tasting. Good Luck!" She also comments,"... if you like, you can add one of these flavors: Coca cola, beer, wine.

Lola W. Taylor

Commentary:
   This is my sister-in-law Lola's original recipe, just as she shared it with me. I was all ready to test it and "Fix it up" with the proper measurements until my friend Nancy gave me the following advice.
   "Why not leave it just as it is? You'll never be able to get the measurements to suit everyone. I'd attempt to make that sauce from the recipe, just as she wrote it!"
   I decided that Nancy was right! So here it is. As Lola says: "Keep tasting and Good Luck!"

E.M.W.

Bum Bye

Hot Biscuits
Butter
Syrup

When we lived in Youngstown, Ohio, years ago, we had a coal stove with a warming oven atop the stove. When Mama had to go out before I came home for lunch she would sometimes leave one of my favorite dishes. She called it my "Bum Bye." She would butter two hot biscuits, lay them in a plate and pour Alaga (Alabama-Georgia) syrup over them. Then she placed the plate in the warmer. I loved it.

Mary Carter Smith

Diet Blues

>Dieters are people
>Who eat more than they want
>They're bothered most by luscious foods
>That beckon, call and taunt.
>Those who diet as they should
>Grow thinner day by day
>But those who cheat and eat and eat
>Grow **FAT** and stay that way!

Elmira M. Washington

Carrot Salad Delight

1 lb carrots, grated
1/2 lb raisins
1 cup coconut, flaked
1 20 oz. can pineapple, drained
1 tbsp. sugar
1 cup whipped topping
1 small can mandarin oranges
1/2 cup pecans (optional)

DIRECTIONS:
Combine all ingredients. Chill
Serves 8

Josephine Wing-Shelton

COMMENTARY:
If you look at the ingredients carefully, you'll understand why we needed a Bits n' Pieces category. I was really in a quandary about which category it should fit.

Use it as the part of the meal you deem best. It is versatile!

E.M.W.

Cucumber Dip

1½ cups cucumber, drained
1 cup sour cream
½ cup salad dressing
½ cup onion, chopped
⅛ teaspoon salt
Dash of pepper

DIRECTIONS:
Combine all ingredients. Mix thoroughly and chill. Crackers and chips for dipping may be served with the dip.
Serves 6-8

Elmira Washington

Dill Dressing

1 cup salad dressing
1 cup sour cream, dairy brand
½ cup milk
¼ cup dill pickle, chopped
¼ cup scallions, sliced
½ teaspoon mustard, dry

DIRECTIONS:
Combine all ingredients. Mix well.
Serves 12-15

COMMENTARY:
This dressing will compliment the 7 Layer Salad recipe quite well. Try it!

Elmira Washington

Incredible Pie Crust

2 cups shortening
2 cups flour
4 teaspoons salt
5 cups flour

DIRECTIONS:
Blend together the shortening, 2 cups of flour and the salt. The mixture should have the consistency of creamed butter and sugar.

Add 5 cups of flour to the first mixture. Use as needed.

Will keep SEVERAL MONTHS on pantry shelf. Use an AIRTIGHT, COVERED BOWL to store the mixture.

Odessa M. Segers

COMMENTARY:
This unusual recipe is the brainchild of Mrs. Segers. Her god-child, Gloria Davis, thought it would fit right into our collection of "Rare and Well Done" entries.

E.M.W.

Jo's Spaghetti
(Home-made Yat Gow Mein)

1 lb. spaghetti, regular or leftover spaghetti
½ to 1 lb. yellow onions
3 eggs, hard boiled slices
3 large or 6 small scallions, chopped
Soysauce to taste
MSG to taste
Meat or seafood, chopped or chunks,
Suggestions: pork, beef, turkey, chicken, shrimp, crab.

DIRECTIONS:
Prepare spaghetti as directed. Saute onions in bacon fat. Pour onion mixture over spaghetti and toss lightly.

Season to taste with soy sauce and MSG. (one is Accent) Add meat or seafood. Garnish with sliced eggs and scallions. (Use a lot of the tops of the scallions)
Serves 15

Josephine Wing-Shelton

COMMENTARY:
Josephine Shelton needed something different to do with her leftover spaghetti one day and this recipe was the result. It is also a great way to use up left-over meat or seafood. Try mixing chicken chunks and shrimp or turkey and pork chunks. Have fun with it.

E.M.W.

Kwanza Salad

2 cups diced cooked turkey
1 cup diced celery
2 red delicious apples, diced
¼ cup golden raisins
1 teaspoon salt
⅓ cup finely chopped onion
½ cup mayonnaise
½ cup sour cream
1 tablespoon orange juice
Salad greens
4 navel oranges, peeled and sliced
2 purple onions, cut in rings

DIRECTIONS:
In a large bowl combine turkey, celery, apples, raisins, salt and onion; stir to blend. In a small mixing bowl combine mayonnaise, sour cream and orange juice. Spoon into turkey mixture; toss well. Arrange on salad greens. Place orange slices and onion rings around the edge of the bowl. Makes 4 to 6 servings.

Venezuela Newborn

Copyright © 1981 By ESSENCE Communications, Inc.
Reprinted By Permission.

COMMENTARY:
It is said that imitation is the greatest form of flattery. Well! I'm sure that this recipe from ESSENCE (our magazine, ladies) has made Mrs. Newborn the most flattered cook in the country!

E.M.W.

Leftover Chili

Leftover chili - which you always have from another meal.
1 box Corn Muffin Mix

DIRECTIONS:
Place leftover chili in a greased casserole. Pour prepared corn muffin mix over chili. Bake at 350° until corn muffin mix is browned. Serve with crisp green salad.
Serves 12

Shirley J. Wing-Shelton

COMMENTARY:
Jo hates to throw away her food. This recipe helps tune up the taste buds when there is an extra bowl of chili left.

E.M.W.

Low Calorie Fruit Salad

Large slice watermelon, diced
½ cantaloupe, sliced
12-15 strawberries, quartered
½ cup blueberries, whole
½ cup seedless green grapes
2 apples, sliced
2 peaches, sliced
2 nectarines, sliced
2 oranges, sectioned
Ricotta Cheese

DIRECTIONS:
Combine all the fruit in a deep bowl. Let it set over night, if possible; the flavors blend well.

When serving, add a tablespoon of Ricotta cheese on top of each bowl.

Other fruits may also be used, for example, pears, pineapple, raspberries or bananas.

If sweetness is desired, try a single envelope of artificial sweetener poured directly over the fruit.

This is very low in calories, but will satisfy your craving for sweets.
Serves 6-8

Elmira Washington
Doris Waters

Sauce for Cold Fruit

¼ cup cornstarch
1 cinnamon stick
½ cup water, cold
2 envelopes EQUAL

DIRECTIONS:
Mix cornstarch, cinnamon stick and Equal with cold water in sauce pan. Heat to boiling; stir until mixture is clear and thick – about 3 minutes.

Use over cold fruit and top with the Ricotta.

COMMENTARY:
This is a wonderful lunch time dessert. Fancied up with a bed of greenery, it can serve as a salad. Be sure to use the cheese. It adds just the touch to give the dish that lovely forbidden look. Then you can dive in and really indulge yourself!

Doris Waters told me about the cheese. The sauce is an added bonus!

E.M.W.

Macaroni and Cheese

3 1/2 cups cold water
1 teaspoon salt
2 cups elbow macaroni
1/2 stick margarine or butter
1 - 8 oz. jar Cheez Whiz
1 10 oz. can condensed milk
4 eggs beaten
4 oz. shredded cheddar cheese

DIRECTIONS:
Boil water, salt and 1 tablespoon of margarine. Cook macaroni until tender, (9-12 min.) stirring occasionally. Next drain in colander. Replace in pot, add margarine or butter, Cheez Whiz, condensed milk and eggs. Bake at 400° for ten minutes. Sprinkle top with shredded cheddar cheese and bake until sides of dish are slightly browned and surface is firm and golden.

Verna Day

Milk and Bread

Hot cornbread
Butter
Buttermilk

DIRECTIONS:
Butter a piece of cornbread. Crumble it into a bowl. Pour buttermilk over it. Eat with a spoon.

COMMENTARY:
This was a staple during my childhood. Mama prepared it, and I still enjoy this simple dish.

Mary Carter Smith

Mix

1 16 oz. jar salt-free, oil-free peanuts
Dried raisins
Wheat Chex
Dried banana chips
Sunflower seeds

DIRECTIONS:
Mix ingredients in amounts to suit your taste. Feel free to add other ingredients as dried coconut, other dried nuts, dates, etc. to create a mixture that suits your taste.

Maisha Elaine Parker

A Happy Home Recipe

4 cups of love
2 cups of loyalty
3 cups of forgiveness
1 cup friendship
5 spoons of hope
2 spoons of tenderness
4 quarts of FAITH
1 barrel of laughter

Take love and loyalty, mix thoroughly with FAITH.
Blend it with tenderness, kindness and understanding.
Add friendship and hope, sprinkle abundantly with laughter.
Bake it with sunshine. Serve daily with generous helpings.

Rose Sachet

Dried rose petals – ½ gal.
Ground orris root
Cinnamon, ground
Cloves, ground
Allspice
Lemon grass
Frankincense
Myrrh
Lavender
Rosemary
Jasmine
Lemon oil
Oil of Ylang-Ylang
Amalcimine Earth

DIRECTIONS:
Gather rose petals. Dry. Sprinkle a little of the other additives until you have a fragrance that is pleasing to your sense of smell. Put into a glass jar (for beauty). Cover jar to preserve fragrance.

COMMENTARY:
While teaching a storytelling class in Pikesville, I met a warm-hearted lady, Susan King. She is an avid herb gardener. She gave me a small jar of the sachet and basic ingredients. Then I went to herb stalls, sniffed, asked questions and added other spices. If you have difficulty obtaining ingredients, you may order them from: THE HERB MAN, James W. Berry, 15368 Mowersville Rd., Shippensburg, PA 17257.

I've begun to grow my own lavender and rosemary. Also you may browse in your local herb shops. This sachet is quite expensive in department stores, so it is good to make your own for personal use and for gifts.

Mary Carter Smith

GROWING HERBS:
Low growing herbs such as chives, parsley and marjoram will grow well in pots or window boxes. They are useful as seasonings or as decoration.

TIPS:
Sow seeds for chives directly in the pot. Soak parsley seeds overnight before sowing. Use a seed box covered with glass to grow marjoram seedlings; transplant the seedlings when they reach two inches in height. Keep soil moist. Place in a sunny window. Provide a cool place, but check for high humidity. Use a combination of sand, soil and leaf mould.

E.M.W.

Sherried Custard Sauce

2 egg yolks, beaten
2 tablespoons sugar
¾ cup milk, 1 tablespoon cream sherry
½ teaspoon vanilla
Dash of salt

DIRECTIONS:
In a small heavy saucepan combine egg yolks, sugar and salt. Add milk.

Cook and stir over medium heat till mixture starts to thicken and coats a metal spoon. Remove from heat.

Pour custard sauce into a bowl and set in a larger bowl of ice water to cool. Stir sauce for 1-2 minutes.

Stir in the cream sherry and the vanilla. Cover and chill.

Makes one cup.
Serves 1-2

Elmira M. Washington

Stuffing Outside of the Turkey

Raisins
Croutons
Onions
Celery
Poultry Seasoning
Sausage
Amounts of each ingredient will vary depending on the number of persons to be served.

DIRECTIONS:
Day before soak raisins to produce wine flavor. Saute onions and celery. Blend in sausage. Add croutons. Mix raisins and currants.

Blend all the ingredients and pour the juice from the turkey over them. Bake in oven long enough to heat and bring out the flavor.

William Mumby, Sr.

COMMENTARY:
Priscilla Marshall wrote this note to accompany this recipe.

"This world - famous recipe has been used for some of England's royalty. Mr. Mumby spent thirty years at sea as a chief chef, visiting all continents except Australia."

E.M.W.

Especially For Children

Potato Press

MATERIALS:
Small knife (Parents only)
Potato
Cutting board
Brush
Paint, colored ink, markers
Heavy paper or cloth to print

DIRECTIONS:
Cut potato in half. Draw a pencil design on the potato. Cut out the potato that surrounds the design. Make the design stand out (¼ inch). Dip the potato design into paint (water colors are best) OR Brush paint right on the potato design. Press (lightly, lightly) the potato design onto your paper or cloth. Use a SAMPLE the first time — when you are satisfied with the look of your design, start on the item you are making.

TIPS:
The potato design needs REPAINTING every time! MAKE YOUR OWN DESIGNS WITH THE POTATO PRESS - overlap or crisscross or turn different ways.

Sculpture With Dough

DOUGH RECIPE:
1 cup salt
2 cups flour
1 cup water

DIRECTIONS:
Mix all ingredients, adding water a little bit at a time. Knead the mixture until it has a smooth consistency (like silly putty). Roll the dough to the thickness you need.

COMMENTARY:
Items you can make include jewelry, ornaments for display and decorating, and pictures for framing or wall hangings.

When the item is completed (remember to include holes) bake them on cookie sheets at 325° until they change to a light tan color. Then cool the item and paint or decorate as you see fit. NO EATING ALLOWED!

Elmira M. Washington

Summer Solar Bowl

Line a stainless steel mixing bowl with foil (use heavy duty foil). Set the bowl outside where it can catch the direct rays of the sun; put a rock or board underneath to tilt the bowl toward the sun. Focus the sun's rays to the inside of the bowl to create a cooking surface. Top crackers with cheese and place inside the bowl. When cheese melts, remove and eat.

Toasted Pumpkin Seeds

INGREDIENTS:
pumpkin seeds
1 tablespoon salt
1 ½ cups water

DIRECTIONS:
Wash the seeds free of all pumpkin. Mix the salt and water; soak the seeds in the solution (short time for less salty taste; long time for more salty taste).

Drain seeds on absorbent paper. Spread seeds out on a cookie sheet. Bake the seeds in oven at 350° until they are dried and toasted all over.

Remove from oven and cool. Crack outer shell, remove it and eat!

Elmira M. Washington

Breads

Sandwiches

When Mama's gone
I make my own sandwiches
Mustard
Mayonnaise
Bologna
Peanut butter and jelly
Fancy these sandwiches may not be
But they sure taste good to me

                              Mary Carter Smith
                              ©1976

Where you have once set your cooking-pot throw no stones.

Do not feast on both sides like the knife.

The small piece (of food) is not so small that it will pass by the mouth.

African Proverbs

Fancy Cornbread

1 box Flako corn muffin mix
1 can cream style corn, 1 lb. size
2 eggs, slightly beaten
1 stick melted butter
1 8 oz. container sour cream

DIRECTIONS:
Just dump into bowl, mix, pour into heavy greased pan. Bake at 350° until browned.

Joan M. Stevenson

COMMENTARY:
This bread is easy to make and DELICIOUS! Even after it gets cold, you can reheat it and it's still mouth-watering.

M.C.S.

Pumpkin Bread

3 cups sugar
1 ½ tsp. salt
2 tsp. pumpkin spice
3 ½ cups flour
1 tsp. baking powder
2 tsp. baking soda
2 cups pumpkin (1 small can)
1 cup oil
⅔ cup water
4 eggs, beaten
½ cup walnuts, chopped (optional)
½ cup golden raisins (optional)

DIRECTIONS:
Combine 6 dry ingredients in sifter. Combine first 4 liquid ingredients. Mix dry ingredients in liquid mixture, sifting and beating until batter is smooth. Add raisins and walnuts.

Pour into 2 large loaf pans. Bake at 350° for 1 hour, 20 minutes. Bread is done when loaf shrinks from sides of pan. Smaller loaves require less baking time.

This recipe can be doubled or tripled. The bread freezes well.

Lillian Fleet

COMMENTARY:
Lillian, another of my sisters-in-law, sends us loaves of this marvelous bread. She makes it in big batches and the family members can usually find a loaf in the freezer in a pinch.
  I made this recipe using:
    1 ¾ - 2 cups sugar
    2 ½ cups flour
  It works!

E. M. W.

Quick Zucchini Bread

3 eggs
2 ¼ cup sugar
2 cups grated zucchini (peeled)
3 cups sifted flour
1 tablespoon cinnamon
1 cup nuts or raisins (optional)
1 ¼ teaspoons baking powder
1 cup oil
1 teaspoon vanilla
1 teaspoon salt
1 teaspoon baking soda

DIRECTIONS:
Beat eggs. Continue beating and add oil, sugar, zucchini, and vanilla. Sift dry ingredients and add to first mixture. Fold in nuts or raisins. Spoon into 2 greased and floured loaf pans. Bake at 350° for 1 hour or until golden brown on top. Cool bread on rack. Delicious as just bread. Freezes well. Serves 8

                                                      Priscilla Marshall

COMMENTARY:
Priscilla says you'll be a very popular member of the family if the youngsters can depend on you to have loaves of this bread ready on short notice (or no notice). It travels well too. For instance, it goes quite well with college-bound folk.

                                                              E.M.W.

Refrigerator Rolls

¾ cup shortening
1 cup boiling water OR
1 cup scalded milk
3 eggs, beaten
¾ cup sugar
2 teaspoons salt
1 cup cold water
2 cakes yeast
½ cup lukewarm water
7 ½ cups sifted flour (sift flour TWICE)

DIRECTIONS:
Combine shortening and boiling water; stir until shortening is melted.

Combine eggs, sugar and salt and beat in cold water.
Soften yeast in lukewarm water. Combine the three mixtures and add flour.

Cover and chill overnight. Shape. Let rise under cover in a warm place; use greased pans.
Bake at 400° for 15 minutes.
Makes about 3 dozen.

Gloria Davis

Eggs

Breakfast

Ma gives me bacon and eggs
The kids next door
Go to the corner store
For Pepsi and cake
Ma says mine is more nutritious
I know theirs is more delicious

　　　　　　　　Mary Carter Smith
　　　　　　　　©1976

The man with meat seeks fire.

The nose does not know the flavour of the salt.

He who gnaws the bones knows how he will swallow them.

                                           African Proverbs

Confetti Omelette

6 slices bacon
⅓ c. chopped onion
8 eggs, slightly beaten
1 c. milk
2 tbls. chopped pimiento
1 tbls. chopped parsley
½ tsp. salt
1 c. (4 oz.) shredded sharp cheddar
1 c. (4 oz.) shredded natural Swiss
1 tbls. flour

DIRECTIONS:
Fry bacon until crisp, drain, reserve 1 tbls. fat. Crumble bacon. Cook onion in bacon fat until tender. Combine onion, bacon, eggs, milk, pimiento (optional), parsley and salt. Toss cheddar and Swiss cheese in flour; add to egg mixture. Pour into 1 ½ quart casserole. Bake at 350° for 40 minutes. Serve immediately.
Serves 6

Nancy Peverley

From "The Milkmaid and Her Pail" by Aesop
Do not count your chickens before they are hatched.

Deviled Eggs

1 dozen eggs, hard boiled
2 tablespoons Miracle Whip
¼ teaspoon Old Bay Seasoning
⅛ teaspoon celery salt
⅛ teaspoon onion salt
¼ teaspoon pepper
½ teaspoon Accent (optional)
½ teaspoon dry mustard
½ teaspoon prepared mustard (your favorite)
¾ teaspoon India relish (do not drain)
¼ teaspoon sweet pickle juice
⅛ teaspoon Cayenne (optional) SEE COMMENTARY
Paprika and parsley, prepared or fresh

DIRECTIONS:
Prepare eggs. Slice in half lengthwise. Remove the yolks, being careful to leave whites in good condition. Place yolks in deep bowl; mash with fork. Add all ingredients except paprika and parsley. The mixture will be thick and easy to stir. (If you prefer a thinner mixture, add more salad dressing to taste.) Fill the depression in each halved white with the yolk mixture. A well-rounded tablespoon will fill each white; add more if you wish. Sprinkle filled halves with paprika and parsley flakes.
Serves 8-12

COMMENTARY:
Mary contends that deviled eggs MUST be "HOT" ! (i.e. DEVILED). I included cayenne in my recipe in deference to all of the "hot" food lovers. I'd also suggest that you substitute hot sauce for pickle juice and use spicy mustard.

Mary calls my recipe, STUFFED EGGS ! Feel free to raise or lower amounts of ingredients specified. Use fresh parsley sprigs for garnishing the platter.

Elmira M. Washington

Potato Chip Omelette

4 small potatoes, chipped
1 small onion or ¼ Spanish onion, finely diced
1 or 2 stalks celery, finely diced
¼ cup green pepper, finely diced
2 tsp. parsley flakes or (diced if fresh)
¼ tsp. celery powder (celery salt if desired)
1 tabsp. bacon drippings
Salt and pepper to taste
6 eggs whipped
2 tabsp. milk or cream
Dash of poultry seasoning & curry powder & paprika

DIRECTIONS:
Pare and chip potatoes; chips are made by slicing small, thick pieces. Place in fry pan with onion, celery, peppers, parsley, seasonings and bacon drippings.

Add enough water to cover potatoes. Mix all together, gently. Cook over low heat, uncovered, for 15-20 minutes or until potatoes are tender. **Do Not Overcook.** Most of the water will simmer down. Check for sticking.

Whip eggs in deep bowl, add milk or cream, poultry seasoning and curry powder. Pour eggs over potatoes turning constantly until eggs are cooked. Sprinkle paprika over omelette before serving.

Preparation: time approximately 20-40 min.
Serves 4-6

COMMENTARY:
Necessity in the form of 1 lone potato forced me to find a way to stretch it. I had enough chips after I chipped away at that potato to feed 2 of us. Then I decided to give it a little spirit and I used whatever I found in the vegetable bin to help it along. When the eggs were added, the dish was born.

Elmira M. Washington

Salmon Souffle

1 16 oz. can Pink Salmon
1 cup celery, chopped
1 cup onions, chopped
2 green peppers, chopped
¼ lb. mushrooms, sliced
½ to ¾ stick butter or margarine
Dash of cayenne pepper
¼ tsp. salt
¼ tsp. Old Bay Seasoning
Dash of white pepper
6 - 8 eggs beaten

DIRECTIONS:
Bone the salmon. Add all seasonings to vegetable mix. Saute over low heat, celery, onions, peppers & mushrooms in butter or margarine. **Do Not Overcook.** Mix gently until vegetables are tender, but not brown. Mix salmon with vegetables and let simmer for about 5 minutes. Beat eggs well and pour over salmon and vegetable mixture. Stir lightly until eggs are thoroughly mixed but still fluffy.

Preparation Time: Approximately 30-40 minutes.
Serves 6-8

Irene Holland

COMMENTARY:
Everyone I know has had to put up with me asking for their original recipes. My hairdresser said she couldn't possibly remember what she did when she made one of her "specialties". Then, after listening to me describe one of mine, she told me how she created this recipe. Naturally, I had her repeat the whole thing and here it is, just for you. Enjoy!

E.M.W.

There was once a man who hated EGGS so much that he'd walk miles out of his way if he thought it would give him a chance to insult a chicken.

Meats
Fish
Poultry

Crab Time

Cover the table with newspaper
Take the red crabs from the pot
Hand me a wooden mallet
I like to eat them while they're hot
You must use your fingers
To open them up wide
Then you take out the "dead man"
He's hiding there inside
First you eat the white lumps
Next you crack the claws
Then you lick your fingers
That spicy taste is best of all

                              Mary Carter Smith
                              © 1976

The hand never loses its way to the mouth.

The milker drinks the milk of the first milking.

The son-in-law of a monkey eats what a monkey eats.

                                           African Proverbs

African Chicken

4 medium onions
1 sweet green pepper
6 stalks celery with leaves
some peanut or vegetable oil
2 cut-up frying chickens
salt and pepper to taste
about 12 oz. peanut butter

DIRECTIONS:
Coarsely chop onions, green pepper and celery. Saute in about 4 tablespoons of oil. Into large pot (preferably iron) pour enough oil for deep-fat frying. (about 2 inches deep) Sprinkle salt and pepper on chicken. Cook it in hot oil until done. Remove chicken and pour off oil. Replace chicken in pot and add vegetables. In a separate saucepan slowly add hot water to the peanut butter until it becomes liquified, beating as you mix to prevent lumping. Pour peanut butter liquid into pot with chicken and vegetables. Simmer slowly until tender. Place pot into a larger pan containing water so mixture won't stick. Stir often. Serve with rice.

COMMENTARY:
Many years ago while at Fellowship Farm near Pottsville, Pa. I met a lady from Sierra Leone. I no longer remember her name. She gave me this recipe. This was my first African recipe and many of us have enjoyed this dish over the years. This was when Fellowship House, then on West Preston Street, was the only place I knew where people of different colors and ethnic groups met in a social setting.

Mary Carter Smith

Apricot Chicken

1 chicken cut into parts or 12 chicken wings (fold wing tips under)
1 envelope Lipton's Onion Soup Mix
1 - 16 or 18 oz. jar apricot preserves
⅓ cup of sherry or light wine
(Orange Juice may be substituted for wine)
2 tablespoons brown sugar
3 tablespoons maple syrup

DIRECTIONS:

Fried chicken seasoning (Optional)

Season and place chicken in shallow casserole. Combine rest of ingredients. Pour over chicken. Bake 350° - 45 minutes. (Temperature and time must be adjusted for electric oven)
Serves 4

A. Katherine Gross

COMMENTARY:
"Kitty" Gross would not take credit for this recipe. She said she has "fiddled" with the one she started out to cook and this recipe is the result. I'm just happy that she was generous enough to share the music.

E.M.W.

A TURKEY was trained to drive a school bus. It only had one accident and that was caused by some smart-aleck boys who egged the bird into playing chicken.

Barbecued Chicken & Spareribs

For both:
Salt
Black pepper
Red pepper
Powdered ginger
Garlic powder
Onion powder
Celery salt
Season All

DIRECTIONS:
Line baking pan with aluminum foil. Grease foil lightly.

Chicken
Cut a fryer into pieces. Wash. Pat dry. Lay pieces in pan. Sprinkle spices on pieces. Rub spices into pieces. Turn pieces over so both sides of each piece is coated.

Spareribs
Buy lean spareribs. Have butcher crack and cut into pieces four-five inches in length. Cut off any excess fat. Wash. Pat dry. Lay pieces in pan. Sprinkle spices on spareribs. Rub spices into each piece. Turn pieces over so both sides of each piece is coated.

Both
Place chicken or spareribs in foil-lined pan. Pre-heat oven to 350°. Bake until browned and tender to taste. Some prefer to eat chicken or spareribs at this stage, simply baked. Others place chicken or spareribs in pot containing barbecue sauce. (See Nowden's Barbecue Sauce.) Simmer atop stove under low light about 30 minutes. You may cook a shorter or longer time depending upon individual tastes. Stir occasionally so meat does not stick.

Mary Carter Smith

Bernardo Crab

4 whole chicken breasts, boned
1 cup mayonnaise
1 beaten egg
1 tablespoon minced green pepper
1 tablespoon melted butter or margarine
1 teaspoon minced red pimento
½ teaspoon dry mustard
¼ teaspoon MSG
⅛ teaspoon pepper
Salt to taste
1 pound backfin crabmeat
½ cup mayonnaise
3 or 4 drops Worcestershire sauce
3 to 4 drops lemon juice
Paprika

DIRECTIONS:
Cut breasts in half and cook in oven.
Mix together mayonnaise, egg, green pepper, butter, pimento, dry mustard and MSG, pepper, and salt. Measure ¼ cup of the sauce you just made and set it aside to use later. Combine the remaining sauce with the crabmeat. (This mixture can be refrigerated at this time.)

Flatten the breasts (8) and divide the crabmeat mixture evenly on each one. Bake at 425° until crabmeat starts to become golden brown; about 5 to 15 minutes.

Mix together the remaining sauce with ½ cup mayonnaise, Worcestershire sauce and lemon juice. Place some sauce on each chicken breast and sprinkle with paprika.

Return to the oven for 3 to 7 minutes.
Serves 8

Nancy Peverley

Brule Jol
(West Indian Cod-Fish)

8 oz. dried (salt) codfish
1 small chopped onion
2 medium tomatoes, chopped
1 ripe avacado
tabasco (optional)
lettuce leaves
1 tbsp. salad oil
juice of one lime
1/8 green or red sweet pepper chopped
1/2 tea. white or black pepper
lemon juice

DIRECTIONS:
Soak fish overnight to remove salt. Clean and shred fish. Be sure to remove all bones and skin. Squeeze all water from fish. Mix chopped tomato, onion, pepper and shredded fish in bowl. Marinate with salad oil and lime juice. Add tabasco to taste. Serve on lettuce leaves with slices of avacado. Sprinkle avacados with lemon juice to retain color of avacados.

Rita Cox

COMMENTARY:
There are a large number of blacks from the islands of the Caribbean living in Toronto, Ontario, Canada. This recipe came from Rita Cox, Chief Librarian of Parkeville Library in Toronto. Rita is a native of Trinidad. She served Brule Jol at breakfast with scrambled eggs and halved cherry tomatoes. She had no explanation for the name of this recipe. It is a favorite West Indian dish.

M.C.S.

Buttered Shrimp

Use shrimp in shells.
1 pound shrimp
½ cup vinegar (1½)
½ stick butter (1½) or margarine
2 tablespoons (6) Old Bay seafood seasoning
½ teaspoon salt (none)
Measurements in Parentheses for 5 lbs.

DIRECTIONS:
Melt the butter or margarine in the steamer. Add all the other ingredients. Bring to a boil. Let simmer for 5 minutes. Reduce heat. Add shrimp to liquid and simmer over medium to low heat for 45-50 minutes. Shrimps are done when they turn pink.
Serves 4 (8)

COMMENTARY:
Those of you who do not want or like your shrimp directly in the sauce can use the shelf pan for a crab steamer and the shrimp will have the same flavor, but they will be drier.

Those of you who want the full buttery flavor, have napkins ready; your fingers get kinda messy when you shell the shrimp to eat them.

Don't say you weren't warned. It's worth all the trouble and effort.

Elmira M. Washington

Chicken and Cabbage

4 chicken breasts, halves with skin off
OR
4 whole chicken legs, skin removed
1 medium head cabbage, coarsely shredded
2 cups tomato juice
1 large onion, sliced for rings
1 teaspoon pepper
1 teaspoon salt
1 teaspoon Italian seasoning
½ cup water
1 tablespoon oil
1 garlic clove, minced

DIRECTIONS:
Saute onions and garlic lightly in oil (to bring out flavor.)

Add tomato juice, seasonings, cabbage. Bring to a gentle boil. Add chicken; spoon some cabbage over the chicken.

Lower heat, **Cover** and **simmer** until chicken is done. (about 40 minutes)

Check ocassionally and stir gently to prevent sticking.

Other vegetables which might be used include: mushrooms, green peppers, lima beans string beans, etc. DO NOT USE LEAFY VEGGIES!
Serves 6-8

Doris Waters

COMMENTARY:
We were visiting with Doris and she kindly volunteered to let us "try" her chicken and cabbage. Grand main dish. Next day, my husband finished off the cabbage and declared it to be better than the day before.

E.M.W.

Chicken Noodle Bake

8 oz. uncooked egg noodles, flat
3 cups cooked chicken, diced (3 lb. fryer)
12 oz. sharp cheddar cheese, shredded
2 10½ oz. cans Cream of Chicken Soup
1 cup milk
2 3 oz. cans mushrooms, drained & chopped
½ cup pimento, chopped (OPTIONAL)
1 teaspoon prepared mustard
1 cup soft breadcrumbs; (4 slices)
2 teaspoons butter or margarine, melted. Salt, pepper to taste

DIRECTIONS:
Cook and drain noodles. Combine noodles with all other ingredients except bread crumbs and butter or margarine. Turn into greased 3 quart casserole OR 13 x 9 baking dish.

Combine breadcrumbs and butter or margarine. Sprinkle over top of chicken mixture. Bake at 350° for 1 hour.

Joan Kraft

COMMENTARY:
Joan served this dish when I was visiting her. It is a smooth, creamy, thick, stew-like dish; tastes wonderful.

The recipe Joan used has some resemblance to this one. She did some changing. I liked what Joan did, so I've used her version.

E.M.W.

Chicken Pie

2 cups boiled chicken, cubed
4 tablespoons butter or margarine
4 tablespoons flour
⅛ teaspoon cayenne
½ teaspoon thyme
2 cups chicken stock, heated to warm
Bisquick

DIRECTIONS:
PRE-HEAT OVEN TO 450°

Add butter or margarine to chicken; cook 5 minutes, stirring constantly.

Add flour; when well-blended, add warm stock and simmer 10 minutes.

Season with salt, cayenne and thyme. Pour in baking dish. Make Bisquick rolled biscuits and place on top of chicken mixture. Bake until biscuits are golden brown.
Serves 4-6

Frances Branch

COMMENTARY:
Frances commented that **Everybody** knows how to put together a chicken pie! I, on the other hand, have a notion that everybody will welcome a change or an additional ingredient or a good recipe for chicken pie! Well, here's the answer to all those needs.

E.M.W.

Chicken Pot Pie

FILLING:
½ cup cold chicken broth
⅓ cup flour
1½ cups hot chicken broth
2½ cups stewed chicken (diced in large pieces)
¾ cup drained canned peas
¾ cup sliced celery
1 teaspoon salt

PASTRY:
1 cup all-purpose flour
1½ teaspoons baking powder
¼ teaspoon salt
3 tablespoons butter
⅓ cup milk

DIRECTIONS:
Make a paste by blending cold chicken broth and flour until smooth. Add paste to the hot chicken broth and cook over direct heat, stirring constantly until sauce boils and thickens. Combine with chicken, peas, celery and 1 teaspoon salt, and pour into a 6-cup buttered casserole.

Sift the 1 cup flour, measure and resift 3 times with baking powder and ¼ teaspoon salt. Cut in butter with a pastry blender or 2 knives, then add milk, all at once, stirring quickly with a fork until dough just stiffens. Turn dough out onto floured board, knead half a dozen times, then roll out to make a circle about 8½ inches in diameter, or to fit top of casserole, and about ¼ inch thick. Make several gashes near the center to allow steam to escape then lay on top of the chicken filling. Crimp edge of dough, pressing it firmly against edge of casserole. Bake at 425° for 20 to 25 minutes or until nicely browned.
5 servings.

Dewildera Willoughby

Cousin George's Chicken

½ sweet green pepper (chopped)
1 onion (chopped)
2 stalks celery (chopped)
chopped red, hot pepper or dried hot pepper to taste
salt, pepper, Season-All to taste
1 large frying chicken
1 can Cream of Mushroom Soup (10½ oz.)

DIRECTIONS:
Cut chicken in pieces. Wash and pat dry. Sprinkle with salt, pepper and seasoned salt. Lay pieces in greased baking pan or fryer. Scatter chopped green pepper, onion, celery and hot pepper over chicken. Pour Cream of Mushroom Soup over chicken and seasonings. Cover pan with aluminum foil so that no steam escapes. Place into oven. Cook at 325° until tender, usually 1½ to 2 hours.

George Stevenson

There is a passle of jokes about how the preacher loves chicken. Here is one from our family:

Everyone was putting on best manners because Rev. Johnson was coming to dinner that Sunday. Mama had fried a big platter of chicken, and told Rev. Johnson to help himself. Papa watched as Rev. Johnson took the choicest pieces, and each time he said, "Reverend, help yourself." But as he watched Rev. Johnson take the last good piece, a breast, off the platter, leaving only the bony pieces, Papa said, "Rev., help your DAMN self!"

Curried Stove-Top Chicken

8-10 pieces of chicken, any parts
½ cup celery, diced
½ cup onions, diced
½ cup green pepper, diced
1 tablespoon curry powder
1 bay leaf
Salt and pepper to taste
Dash of poultry seasoning

DIRECTIONS:
Wash and clean chicken. Prepare vegetables. Set aside. Heat 2 cups water to boiling in cast iron skillet. Add all seasonings to boiling water and let simmer until water is half gone. Add more hot water, bring to boil. Then add all chicken pieces and vegetables. Cover pan and lower heat to medium and let food simmer for 20 minutes or until chicken is tender.

Check Chicken Often To Prevent Sticking. Add Hot Water If Needed. The simmering will help a chicken sauce to form and thicken as the chicken cooks. Remove bay leaf before serving. Preparation time: Approximately 40 minutes.
Serves 4

Joi L. Washington

COMMENTARY:
This is a perfect recipe for the working person. Joi created it one day when she was too tired to fry, broil or bake. The chicken tastes delicious fixed this way.

E.M.W.

A chicken and a hog were walking down a country road when they observed a sign. COME TO THE FIRST BAPTIST CHURCH'S HAM AND EGG BREAKFAST TO RAISE MONEY FOR THE BUILDING FUND. The hen said proudly, "I'm making a contribution to that breakfast." The hog said dolefully, "Yes, you're making a contribution, but I'm making a real sacrifice."

Fish and Okra

½ cup peanut oil
1 lb. frozen fish fillets
 (flounder may be used)
3 medium sized tomatoes
1 box frozen whole baby okra (10 oz.)
½ cup water
Season-All to taste
Salt to taste
Pepper to taste
Red pepper powdered or hot sauce to taste
½ cup corn meal

DIRECTIONS:
Pour oil into skillet, heat. Separate fish fillets. Sprinkle with salt, black pepper and sprinkle with corn meal. Brown fillets in oil on both sides, then pour off excess oil. In saucepan pour water on frozen okra pods. Add cut up tomatoes and spices. Cook slowly until okra is tender (about 15 minutes). Place vegetables over fish. Steam a few minutes. Serve hot.

Liberia
Mary Carter Smith

Fried Chitterlings

5 pounds chitterlings
2 medium onions, coarsely chopped
1 teaspoon crushed red peppers
2 teaspoons seasoned salt
3 cups water
2 cloves garlic, sliced
2 eggs, beaten
Cereal or cracker crumbs
Cooking oil

DIRECTIONS:
Clean the chitterlings; discard excess fat and wash thoroughly. Use cold water for several washings. Set aside to soak - about 1 hour, then drain off water.

Place all ingredients in a large pot and cover. Bring to a boil, then lower heat and cook 3 hours or until chitterlings are tender.

Remove from heat; drain well. Pat dry with paper towels and cut into small pieces. Over medium heat, bring cooking oil to high heat.

Dip chitterlings into beaten egg and crumbs. Fry in fat until golden brown. Drain well on absorbent paper. Serve with hot sauce or vinegar.
Serves 4-6

                                                                  Charlotte Little

COMMENTARY:
Back in 1971, Mrs. Little published some of her family recipes as classic examples of "Soul Food." They **are** classics. We are in your debt for helping preserve this part of our heritage, Mrs. Little. Thanks. Now you can understand why I call myself a "packrat;" I saved the whole booklet.

                                                                    E.M.W.

Grilled Shrimp Catonsville

16-20 jumbo shrimp, dehulled, deveined and drained
½ cup onion, finely diced
1 cup catsup
2 tablespoons brown sugar
½ teaspoon salt
¼ cup malted vinegar
½ tablespoon dry mustard
¼ cup fresh lemon juice
¼ cup Worcestershire sauce
¼ cup green pepper, chopped
Seasoned salt & seasoned pepper

DIRECTIONS:
Season prepared shrimp with seasoned salt and pepper; let set at room temperature for 1 hour.

Combine all other ingredients; blend and set over low heat for 30 minutes. Remove from heat and let thicken and cool. Place shrimp in a shallow pan; cover with the cooled sauce and refrigerate overnight.

Set out at room temperature 2 hours prior to cooking. Grill shrimp over very HOT charcoal fire until done; turn and coat frequently with sauce while cooking.

Serve immediately!
Serves 4-6

Earl Kidwell

COMMENTARY:
This man can "burn!"* He was most gracious in sharing his original recipe for grilled shrimp. Said this is one way to put Catonsville on the map. The people who tasted these shrimp say it is already there!

E.M.W.

*Cook

Heart Chop Suey

1 small beef or 2 veal hearts
¼ cup butter or bacon fat
4 medium onions, sliced
1 small stalk celery, diced
2 cups meat broth or
2 bouillon cubes in 2 cups water
¼ cup flour
½ cup cold water
Salt and pepper to taste
2 tablespoons soy sauce or Worcestershire
3 or 4 cups boiled rice

DIRECTIONS:
Split hearts open, remove arteries and veins, then wash thoroughly inside and out in warm water. Drain well. Cut into narrow strips and roll in flour. Brown lightly in melted butter or bacon fat in large heavy skillet or Dutch oven. Add onions and brown lightly, then add celery and enough meat broth or bouillon to cover. Cover tightly and simmer until meat is tender, about 1 hour. Blend flour and water to a smooth paste and stir into chop suey; if gravy is too thick, add a little boiling water. Add seasonings. A little dark molasses or caramel may be added for color, if desired. Serve with hot boiled rice.
5 servings.

Mayner Pope

Imperial Crab and Topping

1 lb. backfin crabmeat
¼ lb. butter
¼ cup onions, chopped
¼ cup green peppers, chopped
1 teaspoon dry mustard
2 teaspoons Worcestershire sauce
1 teaspoon mayonnaise
1 egg, beaten
½ cup cracker crumbs
1 tablespoon parsley flakes
½ cup light cream
salt and pepper to taste
Paprika

DIRECTIONS:
Saute onions and green peppers in butter, until tender. Let cool: add crabmeat and all other ingredients. Mix gently and pack into crab shell dish. Sprinkle with paprika. Broil under medium heat (300° - 325°) about 15 minutes. Remove from broiler and add topping.

TOPPING:
6 egg yolks
1 pint mayonnaise
4 tablespoons Parmesan cheese
Paprika

DIRECTIONS:
After crab is broiled, spoon topping over each dish. Sprinkle with paprika and bake in oven for about 1 (one) minute. Serve hot.
Serves 4-6.

Emmanuel Pennick

COMMENTARY:
The man who gave this recipe to my husband was a Master Chef. If you follow his instructions, you'll have a scrumptious main dish.

E.M.W.

Juicy Hamburgers

7 lbs. ground beef
4 medium onions (chopped)
6 eggs
2 packages dry onion soup mix
1 tbsp. salt
1 tsp. black pepper
Garlic powder to taste
1 tsp. Season-All
1 cup cracker meal
4 cups cold water

DIRECTIONS:
Mix ingredients together. Makes 3 dozen thick hamburgers 3½ - 4 inches in diameter.

Mary Carter Smith

June's and Pie's Pig Feet and Rice

Combine:
8-10 pig feet
¼ cup Worcestershire sauce
½ cup vinegar
5 stalks celery, chopped in large pieces
3 large onions, chopped in large pieces
Salt and pepper to taste; bay leaf

DIRECTIONS:
Cook pig feet in water to cover; add bay leaf and cook over medium heat until tender.

¼ cup soy sauce
¼ cup Worcestershire sauce
3 cans Chinese vegetables
8-10 fresh mushrooms, sliced
1½ tablespoons KITCHEN BOUQUET

DIRECTIONS:
Split the pig feet into 8 sections. Add all ingredients in same pot and let whole mixture simmer over low heat.

2 cups UNCLE BEN'S rice, cooked according to package directions.

SERVE rice with pig feet spooned over it.
Serves 8-10

June J. and Purnell Washington

COMMENTARY:
This brother-sister act pays off in good eating for all of their relatives. They both love to cook and they both love to have others enjoy what they cook. And I do!

E.M.W.

Soul Food

Kosher pickles from a barrel
Pizzas and pig feet
Corn beef on rye
Curly chittlins
Swirly spaghetti
Chicken hot from a deep deep fry
Soul food from behind a counter
Soul food from a corner stall
Soul food from my mama's kitchen
I just love to taste them all

Mary Carter Smith
©1976

June's Shrimp Fried Rice

2 pounds medium-large shrimp, cooked half done and cleaned
1 bunch scallions (green onions), chopped
6 medium carrots, sliced on a slant
1 large green pepper, chopped (medium)
¼ pound snow peas
½ pound fresh bean sprouts
8-10 large mushrooms, sliced
1½ teaspoons garlic salt
¼ cup Worcestershire sauce
¼ cup soy sauce
1 tablespoon KITCHEN BOUQUET
2 cups UNCLE BEN'S CONVERTED RICE
2 tablespoons margarine
5 cups water

DIRECTIONS:

Combine shrimp, vegetables and seasonings in a large bowl. Set aside.

Melt margarine in large skillet or pot; brown the rice; add the water.

When rice has cooked over low heat until the water is almost absorbed, add the vegetable mixture to the rice; continue cooking over low heat until all of the water has been absorbed. ENJOY!
Serves 8-10

June J. Washington

COMMENTARY:
You will definitely enjoy this recipe. I'm a living witness.

E.M.W.

Meat Loaf

1 lb. ground veal
1 lb. ground beef
1 lb. ground pork
1 cup fine dry bread crumbs
2 eggs beaten
¼ to ⅓ cup chopped onion
2½ teaspoons salt
¼ teaspoon dry mustard
⅛ teaspoon celery salt
⅛ teaspoon paprika
¼ teaspoon black pepper

DIRECTIONS:
Combine the 3 meats thoroughly in a large mixing bowl, then work in the bread crumbs. Beat eggs well, add onion and other seasonings and mix well. Add to meat and stir or knead until blended. Pack firmly into a buttered loaf pan, then unmold onto a flat baking pan. Bake in a moderate oven (350°) 1 ½ hours or until well done.
10 servings

Dewildera Willoughby

Mountain Oysters

1 lb. mountain oysters
1 teaspoon salt
1 tablespoon vinegar
1 cup corn meal
½ teaspoon black pepper
½-1 cup vegetable oil

DIRECTIONS:
Have butcher skin and slice oysters. Cover with water and salt and soak for 3 hours. Drain in colander. Place oysters on dish and pat with paper towel to absorb excess water. Put cornmeal, salt and pepper into a paper bag and shake. Then place sliced oysters in bag and shake until coated. Heat frying pan. Pour oil into pan and heat to high temperature. Place coated oysters in hot oil and fry until crisp and golden brown on both sides. Place on a paper towel to absorb excess grease.
Serve while hot.

Aunt Teady, Sallie Lou Coleman

COMMENTARY:
Mountain oysters, raw clams, and goat's head stew were thought to make the eater more passionate. In parts of the Caribbean Islands women were forbidden to eat goat's head stew. Mountain oysters can be purchased in Baltimore at Belair Market. Once cheap, they now retail for nearly $4.00 per pound. I had seen my Aunt Teady fry them, but did not know exactly what went on before. I met Sarah Hill in Belair Market and she supplied the missing instructions.

M.C.S.

Neck Bones and Rice

2 lbs. neck bones
1 tablespoon salt
1 teaspoon pepper
2 medium onions (chopped coarsely)
2 cups rice

DIRECTIONS:
Have butcher cut neck bones into pieces approximately 4 inches by 2 inches each. Wash neck bones thoroughly. Remove any white marrow between bones on flat side. Barely cover the neck bones with cold water. Add salt, pepper and onions. Boil until just done. Drain liquid and reserve it for use later. Rinse rice. Put 4 cups of reserved liquid in pot with meat and cook rice until tender. If rice looks too dry later, add more liquid from broth you saved. Stir enough to keep rice from sticking.

Mary Day Nowden, my grandmother
M.C.S.

Nigerian Stew

5 pig feet (split)
5 chicken wings (disjointed)
1 lb. frozen shrimp
2 large cans tomatoes
2 boxes frozen okra
2 boxes frozen spinach
Red pepper
Salt
Vinegar
Garlic salt (optional)
3 large onions
½ cup oil

DIRECTIONS:
Boil pig feet in vinegar, water and seasonings until tender. Cut up okra and onions. Cook spinach and drain it. Fry onions and peppers in oil. Add pig feet, wings and other ingredients. Add spinach last. Let simmer.

Henrietta Holliman

COMMENTARY:
Soups, stews and potato greens are usually put over hot rice or other starches such as fufu.

Recipe given to Henrietta Holliman by her son-in-law from Nigeria.

M.C.S.

Oyster Stew

1 pint medium oysters (drain oysters, set aside)
2 ½ cups milk
2 tablespoons butter or margarine
Salt, pepper, celery salt, accent (optional)

DIRECTIONS:
Melt 2 tablespoons butter or margarine in double boiler. Add dash of salt, pepper, celery salt, and a dash of Accent (optional). Pour in milk; heat to just steaming. Add the oysters to the milk mixture; stir occasionally as they cook.

Oyster tips will begin to curl after 2 or 3 minutes. Remove oysters from milk with a slotted spoon when tips begin to curl and pour heated milk over them in the bowl.
Serve immediately.
Serves 2

Elmira M. Washington

Rice With Chicken

8-10 pieces of chicken, seasoned to taste
3 medium onions, sliced
Leaves from several celery stalks
8-12 mushrooms, whole or chopped
1 can chicken broth or 1 pkg. Chicken Cup of Soup.
7 tbsp. soy sauce
½ teaspoon marjoram flakes
1 cup rice, uncooked

DIRECTIONS:
Lightly brown chicken in 1 tablespoon oil. Set aside. Prepare vegetables. Combine onions, celery leaves, mushrooms, soy sauce, marjoram with chicken broth. Let simmer for 5 minutes. Add chicken with oil to broth. Let simmer for ½ hour. Add rice and cover. The rice should be done in 15-18 minutes. Add hot water if needed.
Serves 4

Lola W. Taylor

Request

Ma, let me bring Tania home with me
And Ma, fry a chicken
And make some gravy
And cook some rice
'Cause when teacher asked us
What we had for breakfast
That's what Tania told the class
But Ma
I know
That ain't so
She had cold grits

Mary Carter Smith
©1976

Roast Beef

Preheat oven to 350°
5-10 pound roast of beef
1 teaspoon salt
1 teaspoon pepper
1 small onion, sliced
Hand full of celery tops
½ cup water

DIRECTIONS:
Rub salt and pepper into meat on all sides. Place in an uncovered roasting pan and turn meat over and over until it has browned just the way YOU like it. Add onion and celery tops. Add water and cover; aluminum foil may be used for a cover. Cook until tender. Meat is usually ready to eat if it does not show blood when punctured. If you want the meat less than well done, remove while there is still blood showing in the juice. Bake for about 1 hour. Cool slightly before slicing.

Thomas Taylor

Directions For Trussing Poultry For Roasting

1. Lay the unstuffed bird on its back with the tail to your right. Lift the legs so the drumsticks make right angles with the body, and insert the needle, guiding it to come out at the corresponding place on the opposite side. Leave an end of string several inches long.

2. Fold the wings so the tips lie under the back, turn the bird around. Insert the threaded needle down through the angle formed by the wing at your right; then across the back and up through the angle of the other wing. Cut the cord, leaving a long end.

3. Tie the other end of string at the side of the bird; draw the cord up snugly so as to bring the thighs close to the breast, and tie a secure knot. The body cavity may be stuffed at this point, if a stuffing is being used. Lace opening together using strong tooth picks or small skewers and twine.

4. Next insert the threaded needle between the tendons at the ends of the drumsticks, and continue with same cord.

5. Through the flesh behind the tail, at the point where the oil sac was removed, remove the needle and draw the cord up tight so the drumsticks fit snugly against the body and the ends of the bones close to the tail, thus closing the vent opening.

6. Now insert more dressing (if stuffing is used) through the neck opening, using enough to round out the breast nicely.

7. Fold neck in to the back and tuck it under the cord and the wing tips. Fasten it securely to the back with small skewers.

8. The stuffed and trussed bird, ready for the oven, makes a neat, compact parcel with a minimum of protruding parts to become overbrowned.

For quick removal of the trussing cords before the bird is served, cut the cord opposite the knot and pull it out by the knot.

Alice McGill

Roast Chicken (Old Fashioned)

DIRECTIONS:
Choose a nice plump 4½ to 5½ pound roasting chicken. Singe, then thoroughly clean and wash the bird inside and out, rubbing the skin with baking soda and washing well with cold water. Drain and dry thoroughly; then truss (SEE: Directions for Trussing Poultry) and stuff. Place breast-side down on a trivet or wire rack in an open roasting pan. Brush with melted butter or rendered chicken fat. Bake in a moderate oven (325-350°F.), allowing 40 to 45 minutes to the pound (the larger the bird, the shorter is the time per lb.). When cooking time is half over, turn chicken on its back and brush again with melted fat. As breast, crop and thighs brown, cover with 2 or 3 layers of cheesecloth, which may be fastened with a toothpick. Baste through cheesecloth from time to time with 2 tablespoons melted butter and ½ cup hot water. Remove trussing pin before placing chicken on platter to serve.
5 servings

Susie Knight

COMMENTARY:
You have not eaten real roast chicken until you have prepared the chicken the old fashioned way.

A.P.M.

Roast Goose

DIRECTIONS:
Have neck of goose cut off close to the head. To dress a goose, dip up and down in scalding water several times, then wrap in a piece of wet, hot canvas or a heavy cloth bag. Let steam 10 minutes, then remove feathers and down with a rubbing motion toward head of the bird. Singe, then pat over skin 2 or 3 tablespoons baking soda, rubbing thoroughly to remove all soil. Remove entrails. Wash thoroughly inside and out with clear water, then drain well for 2 or 3 hours. Goose may or may not be stuffed. It will cook more quickly without stuffing. Rub inside with 1½ teaspoons salt. If stuffing is desired, Fluffy dressing may be used, but butter should be omitted because of fatness of goose. Truss by folding the wings back and tying them so cord is drawn tightly across back; tuck neck skin under the cord; tie legs together. Rub 1 teaspoon salt over the skin. Lay breast-side-up in open baking pan. Bake in moderate oven (325° to 350°) for 1 hour. Do not prick the skin. Pour off fat from time to time. (Goose fat makes excellent cookies and pie crust.) Cook until very tender, 3 to 4 hours for a 10 to 12 pound goose. Make gravy with the brown juice and a little of the fat in the bottom of baking pan, using 1½ to 2 tablespoons flour to each 2 tablespoons fat and juice in pan. Blend fat and flour thoroughly. Add water or milk, 1 cup to each 2 tablespoons flour used; cook gravy thoroughly. More water or milk may be used to thin to desired consistency.

Potato dumplings are a good accompaniment for goose, if stuffing is not used.

One-half hour before goose is done, drain off most of the fat and drop the dumpling dough by heaping tablespoons around the goose and bake at the same temperature.

COMMENTARY:
My family used to raise geese. I'm here to tell you that geese can be some of the most cantankerous fowl. I shall never forget how they used to frighten me by hissing and chasing me when I was a child.

We used to save the feathers to fill ticks. Ticks are the fabric case of a mattress, pillow, or bolster.

Alice McGill

Roast Possum With Sweet Potatoes

One opossum (commonly known as possum)
Sweet potatoes - as many as desired
Salt and pepper to taste
1 tbsp. salt
Stuffing of choice

DIRECTIONS:
Skin possum. Discard fur. Clean possum out inside and wash inside and outside thoroughly. Cut off head and feet. Place possum in pot and cover with cold water. Add 1 tbsp. salt, and parboil for 20 minutes. Pour off water. You may roast with or without stuffing. If you use stuffing, have it fairly dry as the meat has quite a bit of grease in it. Place meat in roasting pan with rack so fat can drain while cooking. Place in oven preheated to 350°. Bake about two hours. Peel sweet potatoes. Wash. Pat dry. After meat has baked for 1½ hours season with salt and pepper by sprinkling. Lay sweet potatoes beside possum and bake until they are tender.

Elizabeth Murphy Oliver

COMMENTARY:
Mrs. Oliver comes from Indiana. She advises that wild game should not be used until after frost has fallen. In her state the hunting season does not begin until after November 11.

M.C.S.

Shrimp Meat Sauce

1 cup cubed ham
1 lb. ground beef
1 lb. pork sausage
1 cup chopped onions
1 cup chopped celery
2 tbsp. minced garlic
1 cup chopped sweet pepper
1 tbsp. oregano
1 cup oil
1 tbsp. cumin
2 tbsp. Old Bay Seasoning
1 tsp. basil
1 tsp. rosemary
1 tsp. thyme
2 1 lb. cans tomato sauce
1 lb. Polish sausage, sliced
1 lb. peeled, deveined shrimp

DIRECTIONS:
Heat oil in large heavy pot. Brown ground beef, sausage, and ham cubes in oil. Pour off excess oil. Add onions, celery, and garlic. Saute until tender. Add oregano, cumin, Old Bay Seasoning, basil, rosemary and thyme. Stir. Add two one-pound cans tomato sauce. (Add one more can if you want to "stretch"). Stir again. Bring to boil over medium heat. Simmer for one hour. Stir from time to time. Add sliced Polish sausage and shrimp. Simmer ½ hour more. Cool. Refrigerate overnight to allow flavors to blend. Reheat. Serve over cooked rice or spaghetti.
Serves 8-10 people

Mabel Hubbard

COMMENTARY:
Beside being a wife, mother, a judge who is patient, articulate and fair, Mabel Hubbard is an excellent cook. Although she was born in Detroit, her mother is from South Carolina and her father from Louisiana.

M.C.S.

Souse

4 pig feet, fresh
6 pig ears, fresh
6 pig tails, fresh
Half of a hog head, fresh
2 cups cider vinegar
Sage
Salt
Black pepper
Red pepper
1 tbsp. salt

DIRECTIONS:
Clean out hog head. Wash it and other meats thoroughly. Place in large pot. Add 1 tbsp. salt, 2 cups vinegar and enough cold water to cover. Boil until very done. Cool. Take out all bones, after draining off liquid. Add sage, salt, black pepper and red pepper to taste. Put in loaf pan and refrigerate until meat jells. Slice and serve.

Aunt Teady, Sallie Lou Coleman
M.C.S.

Southern Fried Chicken

DIRECTIONS:
Select a 3 to 4-pound frying chicken. Clean, and coat with salted flour (1 teaspoon salt to ⅓ cup flour). In a heavy deep skillet, heat enough shortening to be ¼-inch deep when chicken is added. If a butter flavor is desired, at least ⅓ should be butter. Start cooking in fairly hot fat placing the thick meaty pieces in first, then the bonier pieces. Fry moderately fast until browned on both sides, then reduce to low heat and continue frying very slowly until done, turning once or twice. If gizzard and heart are to be fried, they should be simmered in water until almost tender before frying; liver will fry in a few minutes without previous cooking. Make gravy from fat left in pan.
5 servings.

Some prefer to cover skillet, sometimes adding water after the first browning. This method is especially good with larger chickens which may be less tender, but it is actually fricasseeing rather than true frying.

COMMENTARY:
Fricassee is a dish made of chicken, veal, or other meat cut into pieces and stewed in gravy.

My mama used to prepare this recipe for Sunday morning breakfast. Of course, homemade rolls, and eight o'clock coffee accompanied the mouth-watering Southern Fried Chicken.

Alice McGill

Steak and Rice

1½ lbs. ground beef chuck or rump
1¼ teaspoons salt
Pepper to suit taste
2 teaspoons grated onion
1 egg, beaten
Melted butter

DIRECTIONS:

Purchase meat in single piece and have it ground once. Combine all ingredients except butter, mixing thoroughly but lightly. On a buttered shallow baking pan, mold the meat into the shape of an oblong or a sirloin or porterhouse steak, making it about 1¼-inches thick and pushing edges up so they will be square like a steak. Brush top and sides with melted butter and place in hot oven (450°). Bake 10 minutes, then reduce heat to moderately slow (325°), to finish cooking, which will take about 25 minutes longer. Brush with butter once or twice during baking. Slide carefully onto hot platter, using pancake turner. Serve with tomatoe sauce if desired or with more melted butter.
5 servings.

Susie Knight

Stewed Chicken And Dumplings

3½ to 4-lb. stewing or roasting chicken
2 teaspoons salt

DUMPLINGS:
1½ cups all-purpose flour
3 teaspoons baking powder
½ teaspoon salt
¾ cup milk
1 teaspoon minced parsley (optional)

DIRECTIONS:
Clean chicken by removing all pinfeathers with a strawberry huller or scraping them out with a paring knife, then singe. Rub skin well with baking soda and wash off carefully. After draining well, cut up chicken and peel off excess fat. Chicken should not be washed after cutting up; if washing is necessary, do it quickly in cold water. Keep in covered bowl in refrigerator until ready to cook. Drain off water that collects in bowl. Fit pieces of chicken compactly in kettle, sprinkle with 2 teaspoons salt, then barely cover with cold water. Cover closely, heat to boiling then reuce heat to simmering and cook until tender, 1½ to 3 hours depending on age of fowl. Fifteen minutes before chicken is to be served, add dumplings prepared as follows:

Sift flour, measure, and resift 3 times with baking powder and salt. Add milk and stir just until dry ingredients are dampened; then add parsley and stir until well-distributed. Remove cover from stewing kettle. There should be enough liquid in kettle to barely cover the chicken. Dip a teaspoon into the liquid, then into the dumpling batter, and drop a spoonful onto the chicken. Dipping spoon in the hot liquid prevents dough from sticking to spoon. Drop all dumplings in quickly; then replace cover and boil gently 12 minutes. Remove dumplings to platter, and arrange pieces of chicken around them. Pour the thickened liquid into gravy boat and serve at table.
5 or 6 servings

Alice McGill

Sweets

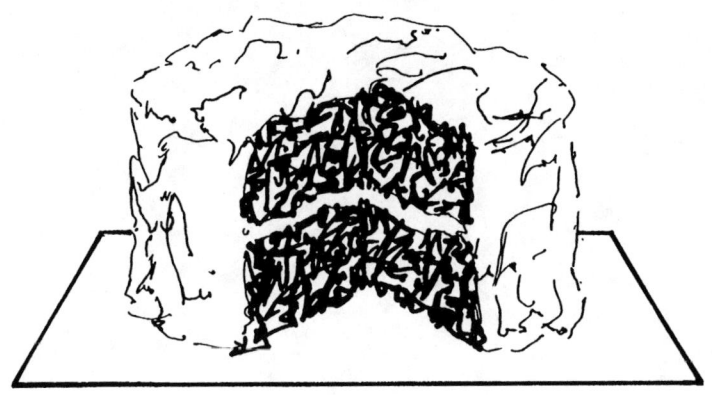

Baker

Get out the pan
Let's make a cake
Set the oven right to bake
Eggs so yellow
Flour so white
Spices and powder
Make a lovely sight
You have to beat it
And beat it
With all your might
Then it will rise exactly right
Making a cake
Is lots of fun
I'm almost sorry
When it's done
But it surely is one of my wishes
Not to wash those dirty dishes

Mary Carter Smith
© 1976

If you have only one cow you don't say, "Which cow gave this milk?"

It is not the pot put on first, but the pot put on the fire (that gets done).

The chicken isn't wiser than the hen.

Dine and recline if for two minutes; sup and walk if for two paces.

African Proverbs

Alabama Coconut Pound Cake

3 sticks margarine
3 cups sugar
6 eggs
1 can (4 oz.) coconut flakes or shreds
3 cups sifted flour
1 tsp. baking powder
1 tblsp. lemon extract
1 cup evaporated milk
¼ tsp. salt

DIRECTIONS:
Cream butter and sugar. Add eggs one at a time, beating well after each addition. Sift dry ingredients together and add alternately with undiluted evaporated milk. Mix in coconut and lemon flavoring. Pour into greased tube or Bundt pan. Bake at 350° for 1 hour and 5 minutes (Maybe a little longer.) When you press cake gently with finger and it springs back, cake is done.

Linda Richardson

Ambrosia

2 cups orange segments
1 cup flaked or shredded coconut
1 cup canned or fresh pineapple tidbits

DIRECTIONS:
Cut oranges in half. Remove seeds. Remove the segments of the orange with a spoon. Squeeze juice from orange halves into a bowl. Add coconut and pineapple. Stir, place in refrigerator.

Variation - add marshmallow tidbits, sour cream and chopped nuts.

COMMENTARY:
Christmas wasn't Christmas without ambrosia. Mama would always make a big bowl for this holiday.

Mary Carter Smith

Autumn Woodlawn Cake

2 sticks butter
4 eggs
3 cups flour
1 cup milk
1 tsp. lemon extract
2 cups sugar
2 tsp. baking powder
Pinch of salt
1 tsp. vanilla

DIRECTIONS:
Cream butter and sugar. Add eggs one at a time, beating well after each addition. Combine dry ingredients and mix in alternately with the milk. Add flavorings. Pour into 2 layer cake pans and bake at 350° for 30 minutes. Allow layers to cool before adding filling and icing.
Serves 12-15

Fred & Harriet McLean

COMMENTARY:
Freddie McLean made me a scrumptious coconut cake once, a long time ago. His wife, Harriet, shared this recipe with us. She wants to be sure that this good old recipe stays with us. We almost lost it when Freddie left us a few years ago, but now we can preserve it.

E.M.W.

Banana Pudding

2 cups milk
2 eggs, plus 2 egg yolks
½ cup sugar
2 tablespoons flour
1 tablespoon butter
1 teaspoon vanilla extract
1 box vanilla wafers
6 bananas, cut in round slices
2 egg whites, beaten stiff
2 tablespoons sugar

DIRECTIONS:
Pour milk into the top of a double boiler. Beat eggs well, then add sugar and flour and blend. Pour the egg mixture into milk and let simmer for 20 minutes stirring constantly. Add butter and vanilla, stir, and remove from heat. In a deep ovenproof dish place a layer of vanilla wafers.

Cover them with a layer of sliced bananas, and pour over them a portion of the custard. Continue layers 3 times. Cover with meringue composed of beaten egg whites and sugar. Then bake in a preheated 375° oven for 15 minutes or until top is golden brown.

COMMENTARY:
This is the traditional recipe for banana pudding. It is delicious!

Mary Carter Smith

Bitsy's Light Fruit Cake

¾ cup butter
2⅓ cups sugar
8 eggs separated
4 cups flour (sifted)
½ teaspoon allspice
2 teaspoons cinnamon
2 teaspoons nutmeg
2 teaspoons ginger
2 packages golden raisins 15 oz.
2 packages currants 15 oz.
2 lbs. diced candied fruit and peels
⅛ lb. broken walnuts
1 cup sherry

DIRECTIONS:
Cream butter and sugar. Beat egg yolks. Add to butter and sugar. Sift flour with spices. Add raisins, currants, fruit and walnuts. These should be well-coated in the flour mixture. Add sherry. Beat egg whites until they are stiff. Batter will be thick. Use your hands to mix egg whites thoroughly into mixture. Grease and flour Bundt or tube cake pan. Pour batter into pan. You may care to decorate the cake by placing whole walnuts and candied cherries on top of batter. Place in 300° oven and bake about 2 hours and 20 minutes.

Gwendolyn N. Samuels

Black Raspberry Cobbler

1 quart black raspberries
½ cup sugar
2 tablespoons flour
1 tablespoon lemon juice
1 cup sifted all-purpose flour
½ teaspoon salt
1¼ teaspoons baking powder
¼ cup shortening
About ½ cup milk

DIRECTIONS:
Wash and drain fruit. Combine sugar and 2 tablespoons flour and mix with berries. Add lemon juice and put in buttered deep pie dish. Sift flour, measure and resift with salt and baking powder. Cut in shortening, using a pastry blender, then gradually stir in milk until dough clings together. Pat or roll out dough ¼-inch thick and place it on top of fruit mixture. Trim edges and cut several gashes in center for steam to escape. Bake in a hot oven (450° F.) 20 minutes, then reduce heat to slow (300° F) and continue baking until berries are cooked through. Plain pastry may be used instead of biscuit dough for crust.
5 servings

Juanita Clark

Blackberries

You start out early
Real early in the morning
You cover your arms and legs
From the thorns
The first berries
You drop in your bucket
Go
PLUNK
PLUNK
But you pick some more
Then they make a soft, soft, sound
Purple fingers
Purple teeth
One for the bucket
Two for me

Mary Carter Smith
© 1976

Cheese Cake

PREHEAT OVEN TO 350°

2 pkgs. cream cheese
⅔ cup sugar
3 eggs
1 teaspoon vanilla
1 teaspoon lemon juice
1 9-inch Graham cracker crust

TOPPING
1 cup sour cream
1 teaspoon vanilla
½ tablespoon sugar

DIRECTIONS:
Cream the cheese; add sugar. Beat well. Add eggs one at a time. Beat well. Add vanilla and lemon juice. Cook for 40-45 minutes or until done. Remove from oven. Apply topping and bake for another 5 minutes at 400°.

Cool before serving.
Serves 8

Joann T. Kelly

COMMENTARY:
This is easy to make and almost foolproof. The taste is great! Joann wrote this recipe out for me back in the 70's.

E.M.W.

Mother-In-Law Cake

1 tall son, well-raised
1 small girl, very sweet
1 mother, filled with love for her son

DIRECTIONS:
Dash of worry. Dash of concern, but not too much. Blend well with heaping cups of love and understanding. Let rise in a room with even tempers and patience.

RESULT:
One daughter, just like the one you always wanted. One happy son and a loving family that enjoys it all.

Nancy Beser

Coconut Pie

¾ cup sugar
2 tbsp. flour
¼ tsp. salt
2 eggs
3 tbsp. melted margarine or butter
1 cup milk
1 cup grated coconut
1 tbsp. lemon flavor

DIRECTIONS:
In a bowl mix sugar, flour, and salt. Beat eggs. Add them. Next add milk, coconut and lemon flavor. Blend well. Pour into unbaked pie shell. Bake at 425° about ½ hour.

Mary Taylor

COMMENTARY:
When I first attended Huber Memorial Church of Christ over two years ago, there were about 15 members there. They were loving people struggling to keep the church alive. To help meet expenses they sold dinners on Saturdays. Mary Taylor, a cook extraordinaire, made many cakes and pies for the church. Her coconut pie is one of her most popular sweets.

We are grateful to now have about 200 members and no longer sell dinners. However, we still have sweets and beverages we serve, without charge on Sundays after service.

M.C.S.

Cold Oven Pound Cake

3 cups sugar
½ cup Crisco
½ teaspoon salt
3 cups flour (cake flour)
1 small can milk (add water to make 1 cup)
2 tablespoons vanilla
Butternut flavoring
2 sticks margarine
5 large eggs

Do not preheat the oven

DIRECTIONS:
Cream the shortening, sugar, salt: Add eggs one at a time. Add flour and milk alternately, ending with flour. Fold in flavoring by hand. Bake in greased tube pan for 1 hour and 45 minutes - 325 degrees*. Start in cold oven. Do not open oven while baking.

*Note - time cake when oven reaches 325°. Softasilk cake flour makes a higher cake.

Virgie Lawson
Marie Foster

COMMENTARY:
Both ladies submitted recipes for Cold Oven Pound Cake.

E.M.W.
M.C.S.

Cream Puffs

½ cup boiling water
¼ cup butter
½ cup all-purpose flour
2 eggs

DIRECTIONS:

Pour boiling water over butter in a saucepan; bring to a boil until butter melts. Now add flour all at once and stir constantly with a wooden spoon until the mixture leaves the sides of the pan and forms a ball. Remove from heat. Immediately add unbeaten eggs one at a time, beating to a smooth paste after each one. Then beat the mixture until smooth and velvety. Drop by heaping tablespoonfuls onto a greased baking sheet, keeping mounds uniform in shape and height, about 3 inches apart. Bake in a hot oven (450°) 15 minutes or until well-puffed and delicately browned. Then reduce heat to slow (300°) and bake 30 to 40 minutes longer; this will bake the centers thoroughly, but puffs should become no browner. Remove to a cake rack to cool. When cold, cut off tops with a sharp knife. Fill with cream filling, thick soft custard, or whipped cream, and replace tops.
6-7 cream puffs

SWAN CREAM PUFFS

DIRECTIONS:

To make the swan neck and head, pipe the choupaste (cream puff mixture) through a large pastry tube, using a large star tube onto the greased baking sheet in the shape of an S; for the tail, pipe a comma-shaped piece. Make one for each cream puff and remove from the oven after the first 15 minutes of baking. After filling the cream puffs, insert a head and a tail in each swan, cutting holes if necessary. The tops cut off to put in filling may be cut in half and stuck into the cream filling at an angle to simulate lifted wings.

Alice McGill

Cream Filling For Cream Puffs

½ cup sugar
¼ cup flour
½ teaspoon salt
1½ cups milk, scalded
1 egg beaten
1½ tablespoons butter
¾ teaspoon vanilla or ½ teaspoon lemon extract

DIRECTIONS:
Mix sugar, flour and salt in top of double boiler. Gradually stir in the hot milk and cook over direct heat until thickened, stirring constantly. Stir a little of the hot mixture into the beaten egg; return this to rest of mixture and place over boiling water, stirring constantly for 2 minutes. Remove from heat, stir in butter and flavoring and cool. Fill into cream puffs or eclairs. For best flavor and crispness, filled cream puffs or eclairs should be served the same day they are baked, and filled puffs should be kept in refrigerator. Enough filling for 5 good-sized cream puffs.

Alice McGill

Five Flavor Pound Cake

2 sticks butter or margarine
½ cup cooking oil
3¼ cups sugar
5 eggs, well-beaten
3 cups flour
1 cup milk
½ teaspoon baking powder
1 teaspoon vanilla extract
1 teaspoon rum extract
1 teaspoon coconut extract
1 teaspoon lemon extract
1 teaspoon butter flavoring

DIRECTIONS:
Cream butter or margarine and oil; add sugar. Mix well. Combine dry, well-sifted ingredients; add to sugar mixture alternately with milk. Add one egg at a time; beat well after each egg. Add flavorings - one teaspoon at a time. Fold in each flavor carefully and mix well.
Grease and lightly flour a tube pan; pour batter around tube evenly. Bake at 325° for 1½ hours.

EXTRA ADDED ATTRACTION (OPTIONAL)
½ cup water
1 cup sugar
1 teaspoon each of the five flavors

DIRECTIONS:
Combine all ingredients; heat to boiling. Pour mixture over hot cake as soon as it is taken from the oven.

Gloria Davis

COMMENTARY:
Gloria recommends this delicious cake for holidays. It keeps well in the refrigerator. Travels well too, due to its moistness.

E.M.W.

Fresh Peach Pie

Plain pastry
2 to 2½ lbs. peaches
2 tablespoons flour
¾ cup sugar
2 tablespoons butter
⅛ teaspoon almond extract

DIRECTIONS:
Make pastry for a double-crust pie. Roll out slightly more than half the pastry and fit into bottom of a 9-inch pie pan. Pare and slice peaches. Place in layers in the pastry-lined pie pan, sprinkling the flour and sugar, mixed together between the layers. Dot top layer with the butter and sprinkle the flavoring over all. Roll out rest of pastry ⅛-inch thick and cut in strips about ⅜-inch wide. Lay over peaches to form lattice crust, placing all the parallel strips across one way and folding back alternate strips as each of the remaining strips is laid in place to produce a woven lattice. Trim off pastry even with pan rim. Bake in a hot oven (450°) 15 minutes, then reduce heat to (325°) moderately slow and bake 20 to 25 minutes longer or until peaches are soft.
6 servings

Alice McGill

Fresh Plum Pie

2 lbs. fresh plums
Plain pastry, double crust
¾ cup sugar
2 tablespoons flour
½ teaspoon cinnamon
1 tablespoon butter

DIRECTIONS:
Wash plums but do not peel. Cut in halves and remove pits. Roll out slightly more than half the pastry to line an 8-inch pie pan, and fit carefully into angles. Trim off pastry even with pan rim. Arrange plums in the pastry-lined pan. Blend sugar, flour and cinnamon and sprinkle over the plums. Dot with butter. Roll out rest of pastry, gash in several places. Moisten edges of lower crust, then lay upper crust over the plums and press upper and lower edges of pastry together. Trim off pastry ½-inch from edge, turn under and flute edge as desired. Bake in a hot oven (450°) 12 minutes, then reduce heat to moderately slow (325°) and bake 25 minutes longer or until fruit is tender. Remove to cake rack to cool. Serve warm or cold.
5 or 6 servings

COMMENTARY:
There was a plum tree on every ditch bank at home in North Carolina. But we could not cook the plums because they were all pit and juice. So we made plum wine which was delicious. My mother bought the cooking plums from the market.

Alice McGill

Fried Orange Delite

6-8 fresh oranges
1 box Orange cake mix
Orange juice as needed
Powdered sugar
Coconut, shredded or flaked
Vegetable oil

DIRECTIONS:
Peel oranges and separate sections. Mix the cake mix and enough orange juice to make a stiff batter. Coat orange slices with batter. Fry batter covered slices in hot oil (350°) until golden brown. Drain the fried slices on paper toweling. Roll fried slices in coconut and powdered sugar. Serve warm.
Serves 15-18

Louis Denson (Wendy Gleason's uncle)

COMMENTARY:
Wendy is a former pupil of mine who has kept in touch even though she and her family now live in Pennsylvania. She said her uncle won a prize with this recipe. It's easy to understand why.

E.M.W.

Friendship Cake

To make one cake

1 box yellow cake mix (or white)
1 box instant pudding mix (pineapple or vanilla)
1 cup chopped nuts
⅔ cup oil
4 eggs
⅓ of the fruit mixture

DIRECTIONS:
Mix all ingredients above. Bake in a greased tube or Bundt pan at 350°. Cake must bake for 70 minutes. Do not use cake tester too soon or cake will fall.

To prepare fruit

7½ cups sugar
1½ cups starter
1 large can sliced peaches and juice
1 large can chunk pineapple and juice, unsweetened
1 large can fruit cocktail and juice
1 10 oz. jar Maraschino cherries, halved

Day 1
    2½ cups sugar
    1½ cups starter
    1 large can sliced peaches and juice
Mix together and stir every day.

Day 10
    2½ cups sugar
    1 large can chunk pineapple and juice, unsweetened
Mix with peach mixture and stir every day.

Day 20
    2½ cups sugar
    1 large can fruit cocktail and juice
    1 large (10 oz.) jar Maraschino cherries and juice
Mix with peach and pineapple mixture and stir every day.

(continued)

Friendship Cake (continued)

Day 30
Drain liquid from fruit. **This is the starter.**

Divide the juice into 1½ cups for each container. Cap containers tightly and give to a friend (with a copy of the recipe) as soon as possible. Divide the fruit into thirds and make three Friendship cakes. You may freeze the cake.

HINTS:
During the 30 days, the fruit mixture should **not** be refrigerated. Keep the fruit mixture in a covered container at room temperature. The fruit mixture will bubble as it ferments; a lightweight lid will pop off. If this happens, simply add a heavy object to weight the lid; the fruit must be covered at all times. Starter juice should **not** be refrigerated. It may be kept up to 20 days before starting a cake.

Lila Powell

COMMENTARY:
Lila Powell gave me recipe and starter. Enjoy!

M.C.S.

Grandmom's Sweet Potato Cake

4 eggs
2 cups all-purpose flour
2 cups sugar
1 cup salad oil
1 can (1 lb.) sweet potatoes (or yams)
2 tsps. baking soda
¼ tsp. salt
½ tsp. ground cloves
2 tsp. cinnamon
½ tsp. ginger
1 tsp. nutmeg

DIRECTIONS:
Preheat oven to 350°.
In large bowl let the eggs warm to room temperature. (½ hour)
Combine dry ingredients in sifter.
At high speed, beat eggs with sugar until light and fluffy. Beat in oil, yams or sweet potatoes to blend well. At low speed, beat in flour mixture just until blended.
Pour into an ungreased 9" tube pan.
Bake about 1 hour or until surface springs back when lightly touched.
Cool completely in pan.
Frost with your favorite icing.

Therese Chambers

Harvest Cake

1 ¾ cups flour
1 teaspoon baking soda
1 teaspoon cinnamon
½ teaspoon salt
½ teaspoon nutmeg
¼ teaspoon ginger
¼ teaspoon ground cloves
½ cup butter
1 cup sugar
2 eggs
¾ cup pure pumpkin (not pumpkin pie mix)
¾ cup Nestle's Semi-Sweet chocolates (mini)
¾ cup walnuts

DIRECTIONS:
Combine flour, soda and spices. Cream butter, gradually adding sugar. Blend in eggs. Beat well at low speed adding dry ingredients alternating with pumpkin. Stir in chocolates and walnuts. Sprinkle top with ¼ cup walnuts. Bake in oven 65-75 minutes at 350°. Let cake stand 6 hours before slicing.

Glaze for Harvest Cake

¼ cup confectioners sugar
⅛ teaspoon nutmeg
⅛ teaspoon cinnamon
1-2 tablespoons cream

Freda Mason

Hot Milk Cake

DIRECTIONS:
Put ¼ lb. butter in 1 cup milk and bring to a boil. Set on side of stove. Beat 4 eggs, add 2 cups sugar and 2 cups flour, then add hot milk and butter mixture; add 1 tsp. vanilla, add 1 large tbs. of baking powder and ⅛ tsp. salt. Bake at 350° in 3 large cake pans about 35 minutes. Frost as desired.

Ruth Ann Zeller

From "The Belly & The Members"   - by AESOP

After a day or two of refusing to work in order to make the Belly do more than just receive food, the Members of the Body found that even the Belly in its dull quiet way was doing necessary work for the Body, and that all must work together or the Body will go to pieces.

Lemon Dainty

3 tbsp. flour
1 cup sugar
3 tbsp. butter
3 eggs, separated
1 cup milk
¼ cup lemon juice
¼ tsp. lemon rind

DIRECTIONS:
Mix flour and sugar. Cream butter and flour mixture. Beat egg yolks and milk. Gradually add lemon juice and rind. Beat egg whites until dry. Fold in carefully. Pour into greased baking dish. Place pan in 1 inch of water. Bake 35 minutes at 350°.

Dorothy Ross

Lemon Meringue Pie

1 9-inch baked, one crust pie shell
1 cup sugar
¼ cup flour
3 tablespoons cornstarch
2 cups water
3 eggs, separated
2 tablespoons butter
¼ to ½ cup lemon juice to taste
grated rind of 1 lemon
dash of cream of tartar
6 tablespoons sugar

DIRECTIONS:

In medium-sized saucepan combine sugar, flour and cornstarch. Gradually stir in water. Bring to a boil and cook, stirring constantly, until thickened.

Gradually stir the hot mixture into the egg yolks, return to saucepan over low heat and cook, stirring for 3 minutes.

Remove from heat and stir in butter, lemon juice and grated rind. Cool slightly, then pour into baked shell. Cool completely.

Make a 3 egg white soft meringue as follows: Beat 3 egg whites until frothy. Add dash of Cream of Tartar and continue to beat until egg whites are stiff enough to hold a peak. Gradually beat in 6 tablespoons sugar and beat until meringue is stiff and glossy. Pile meringue lightly on pie. Bake in preheated oven 425° for 5 minutes or until the high peaks of the swirls are delicately tinted with brown.
Serves six

Mary Carter Smith

Lemon Stack Pie

2 tsp. unflavored gelatin
⅓ cup fresh lemon juice
3 eggs beaten
1¼ cups sugar
1½ tsp. butter
Grated rind of 1 lemon
1 pkg. pie crust - or your own recipe
1 cup whipping cream
Grated lemon (rind for garnish)

DIRECTIONS:
Soften gelatin in lemon juice, Mix with eggs, butter, rind in saucepan. Cook over low heat, stirring, until mixture thickens. Remove from heat: cover, chill until mixture mounds slightly when dropped from spoon.

HEAT OVEN TO 475°. Mix pastry as directed in pkg; make 9" baked pie shell with half the dough. Bake 8 to 10 min. Cool. Roll rest of dough into two 6" rounds. Place on baking sheet, prick, bake 8 to 10 minutes. Cool. Fold half of whipped cream into filling. Spread ⅓ of filling in pie shell: top with baked round, more filling, baked round, rest of filling. Garnish with whipped cream and lemon rind. Chill at least 1 hour.

COMMENTARY:
This is my favorite confection and my favorite recipe. It falls under the category of fattening, as in 'fattening, sinful or immoral.'
Make it once a year or so. More and you'll turn into a lemon stack pie freak!

Elmira M. Washington

Mama's Tea Cakes

1 cup **butter** (other shortening will not have the same taste)
1 cup sugar
3 eggs
1½ teaspoons vanilla flavoring
3½ cups sifted flour
½ teaspoon baking soda
1 teaspoon baking powder

DIRECTIONS:
Cream butter, sugar and eggs. Add vanilla. Sift dry ingredients and add by hand. If necessary more flour may be used to make dough stable enough to knead. Place dough on a floured board and roll out fairly thick. **Do not** roll the dough out thin. Cut out dough with biscuit cutter. Place them on a greased sheet. Do not let sides touch. These tea cakes will be crisp. Bake at 400° until browned.

Mary Carter Smith

Miss Marie's Sweet Potato Pie

3 medium-sized sweet potatoes (I prefer orange-colored)
1½ cups sugar
½ lb. butter
1 teaspoon fresh lemon juice
½ can condensed milk or 1 small can of milk
4 eggs
nutmeg, vanilla and rum flavoring to taste
1 teaspoon baking powder (fold in last)

DIRECTIONS:
Peel and cook sweet potatoes and mash them. Add sugar and butter while hot. Add lemon juice. Next add milk. Consistency will be loose. Eggs are added after mixture has cooled. Add flavorings to taste. Pour into prepared pie shell. Bake at 350° until browned.

Marie Humphrey

COMMENTARY:
Marie Humphrey, known as Miss Marie, was a faithful member of First Baptist Church and a close friend of Aunt Booby. She cared for Aunt Booby and many others who were ill. Her cooking was legendary. She passed in July, 1984 at the age of 91.

M.C.S.

Old Fashioned Carrot Cake

1½ cups WESSON oil
2 cups sugar
4 eggs
2 cups flour
1 teaspoon salt
3 teaspoons cinnamon
2 teaspoons baking soda
2 teaspoons vanilla
3 cups carrots, grated OR pureed in blender

DIRECTIONS:
PREHEAT OVEN TO 325 degrees. Combine oil, sugar and eggs; beat well. Add sifted dry ingredients; beat well. Add vanilla and carrots; stir until smooth.

Grease cake pan. Use layer pans or tube pan or loaf pans.

Bake for 45 minutes or until cake shrinks away from sides of pan. Frost if desired.

Cream Cheese Icing

1 stick margarine
8 oz. pkg. cream cheese
1 box confectioner's sugar
2 teaspoons vanilla

DIRECTIONS:
Cream the margarine and cream cheese. Add sugar till desired consistency is in bowl; add vanilla.

Let icing set before spreading on cake. In summer, you may need to set it in the refrigerator briefly; cream cheese tends to soften as it is used.

REFRIGERATE THE CAKE UNTIL ALL GONE

Rachel K. Baumgartner

COMMENTARY:
This is another of the recipes I received back in the 70's. Rachel's favorite cake recipe was first printed in New Jersey by The Forum School in their cookbook, "Forum Feasts."

E.M.W.

Philly Pound Cake

1½ cups sugar
1 large pkg. cream cheese, softened
1½ sticks butter
1½ teaspoons vanilla
4 eggs
2 cups cake flour, sifted
1½ teaspoons baking powder
Confectioner's sugar

DIRECTIONS:
Combine sugar, softened cream cheese, butter and vanilla; mix until well-blended. Add eggs, one at a time, beating well on low speed.

Mix dry ingredients and add to cheese mixture gradually until well-blended. Grease and flour a 9 x 5 loaf pan; pour batter into pan and bake at 325 degrees for 1 hour and 20 minutes.

Let cool; remove from pan and sprinkle with confectioner's sugar.

Elmira Washington

Plain Cake

1 stick margarine
8 eggs
3 cups flour
2 sticks butter
2 cups sugar
1 tsp. each: vanilla & lemon juice

DIRECTIONS:
Separate eggs. Beat whites until stiff. Refrigerate. Beat egg yolks until thick. Cream butter/margarine. Whip with beater. Mix in sugar – beat until smooth. Add egg yolks. Add flavorings. Fold in whipped egg whites. Check bowl for separation – if separation has occurred during refrigeration, beat whites at bottom of bowl until stiffening returns. Add flour, mix well. Batter will be smooth. Pour into well-greased and floured cake pan, tube pan or 3 layers. Bake at 325°.

Delores Terry
Elmira Washington

COMMENTARY:
My friend, Delores Terry, gave me this recipe. Some of you may have written it down when Mary featured it on her show one Saturday. Delores was a great cook and I've always been grateful that she left me something as marvelous as this cake to remember her by.

E.M.W.

Quick Fudge Brownies

½ cup butter or margarine, melted
2 squares chocolate, unsweetened
1 cup sugar
2 eggs
1 cup flour, sifted
1 teaspoon baking powder
¼ teaspoon salt
1 teaspoon vanilla
1 cup nuts, chopped (Optional)

DIRECTIONS:
Use large saucepan so all ingredients can be mixed in it.

Combine butter and chocolate and melt. Let cool.

Add sugar and unbeaten eggs. Blend well. Add sifted dry ingredients and fold in; add vanilla and nuts.

Spread in greased shallow pan. Bake for 15-20 minutes at 350°.
Yield: 1-½ dozen

COMMENTARY:
Another oldie but goodie. You probably won't need to take these out of the pan. People usually just cut a hunk and keep eating until the pan is empty.

Elmira Washington

7 Up Pound Cake

3 sticks butter
3 cups sugar
5 eggs
3 cups flour
¾ cup 7 UP
2 tablespoons lemon extract

DIRECTIONS:
Cream butter and sugar. Add eggs, one at a time; beat well after each egg is added. Blend in all of the flour; beat well. Add lemon extract.

Using the highest speed on the mixer, beat in 7UP; beat well. Pour into well-greased and floured Bundt pan or 2 nine inch cake pans. Bake at 325° for 1 hour, 20 minutes.
Serves 15-20

Harriet McLean

COMMENTARY:
I never thought Harriet would let me share this recipe. Her cakes are famous. A little hint: try coconut extract. Be brave and you will have a delicious cake.

E.M.W.

Southern Apple Cobbler

1 quart apples, pared and sliced, (4-6 med.)
1-1¼ cups sugar
1 teaspoon vanilla
1 teaspoon nutmeg

HEAT OVEN TO 350°

Pastry
¾ cup flour
¾ cup milk
1 teaspoon baking powder
1 stick butter or margarine, melted

DIRECTIONS:
Sprinkle 1 cup of sugar over apples, set aside. Combine vanilla and nutmeg, pour over apples; carefully mix apples for even spread of the flavors.

Mix together flour, milk, baking powder, ¼ cup sugar, melted butter or margarine and pour on top of apples. Bake at 350° until done.
Pastry will sink down and cook inside apple mix. Recipe may be doubled.
Serves 10

Mozella Blackwell

COMMENTARY:
When I tested this old country recipe, I found it needed about 15 minutes more for browning on top. All of my tasters gave it a rousing "M-m-m, gooood!"

Tip: I used green cooking apples.

E.M.W.

Sweet Potato Pie

8 large sweet potatoes, cooked and whipped with electric mixer.
1 tablespoon baking powder
1 tablespoon nutmeg
2 tablespoons cinnamon
4 eggs
2 teaspoons lemon juice (from bottle)
2 cups sugar
4-6 tablespoons rum (optional)
4 9-inch unbaked pie shells
2 teaspoons vanilla
½ cup milk (if needed)

DIRECTIONS:
Combine and mix with electric mixer; the sweet potatoes, baking powder, nutmeg, and cinnamon. Add to potato mixture the eggs, lemon juice and vanilla. Beat until smooth. Add sugar and beat well. If mixture needs to be loosened, add milk. If desired, add rum. Pour into unbaked pie crust and bake at 350° for 35-45 minutes or until done.
Yield: 4 pies (at least 32 slices)

Vernon H. Mason, Jr.

COMMENTARY:
It was hard to pin my brother down when I wanted to include his recipe. He makes these pies all the time, but he does not measure! He cooks "by eye". I worked very hard to get these measurements and he approves of my portions.

E.M.W.

Sweet Potato Pudding #1

5-6 medium sweet potatoes
3 eggs
1¼ cup sugar
1½ tsp. nutmeg
1½ tsp. vanilla
¼ cup sherry
3 tbsp. melted butter
1 cup milk
Large marshmallows

DIRECTIONS:
Combine and beat eggs, sugar, and milk. Add melted butter. Add and mash sweet potatoes with ingredients until smooth. Add and stir in nutmeg, cinnamon and vanilla to taste. Add ¼ cup sherry and stir thoroughly. Pour into greased 2 qt. baking dish. Sprinkle nutmeg on top of pudding. Bake at 350° in preheated oven for about 1 hr. Remove from oven.
Place 6-8 marshmallows on pudding. Put under broiler until marshmallows are light brown. (a few minutes)

Marjorie D. Washington

COMMENTARY:
Marje and I are married to brothers, so she has shared this lovely pudding with the family members a lot. She brings it to you in a casserole all ready to be eaten. It never lasts past the second day.

E.M.W.

Sweet Potato Pudding #2

1 cup of grated sweet potatoes
¾ stick of melted butter
Start with ¾ cup of sugar after mixing all ingredients together.
Add more sugar if desired.
3 eggs (well beaten)
dash of salt
3 tablespoons of flour
2 teaspoons of vanilla flavor

DIRECTIONS:
Add enough milk to make ingredients soupy (about 1 cup) Pour into buttered dish or pan' Cook at 300-350° until knife comes out clean. To make larger portions, double or triple recipe.

COMMENTARY:
When grating pototoes, take care not to skin fingers.

Alice McGill

Trifle

1 box yellow cake mix. Follow directions for mixing and baking. Bake in loaf pan.
2 six oz. boxes Jello, different flavors. Follow directions for mixing and setting in refrigerator.
1 six oz. French Vanilla Instant Pudding. Follow directions for mixing and setting in refrigerator.
1 12 oz. bowl Whipped Topping, frozen (see #2 below)
1 pint strawberries, fresh (in season) halved.
1 11 oz. can mandarin oranges, drained
1 12 oz. can mixed fruit, chunky style, drained
1 20 oz. can pineapple chunks, crushed and drained
Seedless grapes, halved (optional)
3 large bananas, thinly sliced
1 ½ cups pecans or English walnuts, chopped

DIRECTIONS:
Cool the cake, then slice thinly and place enough slices to cover the bottom of a large punch bowl for the first layer. Whipped topping is placed between each layer.

Add a layer of every ingredient until all ingredients are used. Use your imagination. Placement of fruits may be based on color, for instance ...

TIPS FOR TRIFLE
1. Rum may be sprinkled throughout the layers (optional)
2. Slice the topping as it is layered. It is difficult to slice if thawed.
3. Flaked coconut may be sprinkled throughout layers (optional)
4. Brown sugar may be sprinkled throughout the layers (optional)
5. Garnish the last layer (TOP) using whipped topping and a variety of nuts and or fruits.
6. You may vary the ingredients according to your own taste. For example, at Christmas time, use red and green to compliment the white topping and you'll have a holiday color scheme. Keep refrigerated until ready to serve; portions may be allowed to set briefly before trifle is served.
Preparation Time: It varies from cook to cook.
Serves 15-18

Constance Washington

COMMENTARY:
All of the tips and hints that are included in the recipe came from Connie. She's a great believer in creativity and she wants all you cooks to be as skillful as you can when you "build" your trifle. **Reminder:** Cake should be layered throughout the trifle just as the fruits, jello and topping are layered.

E.M.W.

Unbelievable Peanut Butter Cookies

1 cup peanut butter
1 cup sugar
1 egg, unbeaten
1 teaspoon vanilla

DIRECTIONS:
Combine all ingredients until well-mixed. Drop by teaspoonsful on ungreased cookie sheet; OR roll into small balls and flatten tenderly with your fingers or a fork.

Bake at 325° for 15 minutes.
Yield: 45-50

Odessa M. Segers

COMMENTARY:
Brainchild number 2 for Mrs. Seger. Gloria Davis remembers the scrumptious eating these cookies provided when Mrs. Seger baked them for her and the other children.

E.M.W.

Vanilla Ice Cream

2 cans condensed milk plus 1 additional cup
2 cans water plus 1 additional cup
3½ cups sugar
¾ cup flour or you may use ½ cup cornstarch
⅛ teaspoon salt
6-8 eggs
1 tablespoon vanilla flavoring
2 cups heavy cream

DIRECTIONS:
*Scald milk and water. Combine sugar, flour or cornstarch, salt and eggs. Slowly stir into hot milk. Cook in double boiler until thickened. Cool. Add flavoring and heavy cream. Freeze in ice cream maker.

*Place in pot over low flame until hot, not boiling.

COMMENTARY:
I vary this basic recipe by using other flavors as lemon or rum. I also use fruits, such as crushed peaches, strawberries and bananas. The banana ice cream is most popular with family and friends.

Mary Carter Smith

There was some rivalry between the Baptist and Methodist churches in a small town. One day as the Baptists were freezing some ice cream, it seemed that the ice cream wasn't getting hard fast enough. A deacon said, "Take this churn down to that Methodist church. It's cold enough down there to freeze anything."

Watergate Salad

Recipe: No cooking required. May be frozen. Makes (1) one mold or pan of 12 to 18 servings.

READ ENTIRE SHEET BEFORE MAKING DISH

1 pkg. Instant Pistachio Pudding (4 oz.)
1 20 oz. or 15 oz. can Crushed Pineapple, well-drained.
1 8 oz. bowl whipped topping, softened
1 cup minature marshmallows
½ cup Maraschino Cherries, halved and drained
½ cup chopped nuts (optional, since pudding contains nuts)
Pam or preferred vegetable spray.

Note: This recipe can be increased! Increase all ingredients equally.

DIRECTIONS:
Mix together the pudding and pineapple, stir until all pudding is completely disolved.

Add whipped topping, fold in by hand, blend carefully until all ingredients are pale and smooth.

Mix sliced cherries, miniature marshmallows and if desired, nuts. Lightly spray entire surface of mold or pan with vegetable spray; this will make it easier to remove the salad from its container.

Pour mixture into mold or pan, keep refrigerated until ready to serve.

To keep indefinitely, freeze. If frozen, allow 2 hours in refrigerator to thaw, BEFORE serving.

GARNISH: For additional decoration, use cherries, marshmallows and whipped topping to garnish top of salad. When using a mold, place garnish into the mold, then carefully spoon the ingredients over the garnish.

Elmira M. Washington

Wonderful German Apple Cake

1 cup salad oil
3 eggs
2 cups sugar
1 teaspoon vanilla
2 cups flour
1 teaspoon baking soda
2 teaspoons cinnamon
½ teaspoon salt
1 cup nuts
4 cups sliced apples

DIRECTIONS:
Beat oil and eggs until frothy. Add and blend well the sugar, vanilla, flour, soda, cinnamon and salt. Fold in the nuts and apples.
Bake at 350° for 1 hour in 9 x 13 pan.

Icing

1½ tablespoons soft butter
1 teaspoon vanilla
¼ cup confectioner's sugar
3 ounces cream cheese

DIRECTIONS:
Blend well and spread on the cake as soon as it comes from the oven.

Ruth Ann Zeller

COMMENTARY:
Joan and John Kraft recommend this cake highly.

E.M.W.

An Araber

This farmer raised a TURNIP that weighed 390 pounds. He was so proud of it that he kept it so he could have his picture taken with it. When he posed beside the turnip, somehow he tipped it over and got himself squashed instead!

Vegetables

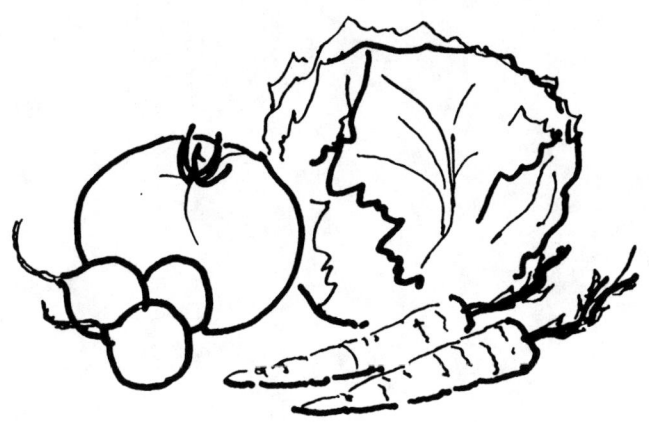

Araber

The Araber comes through our street
His wagon is loaded with things to eat
Red tomatoes
Corn, fresh and green
With little windows so the grains are seen
Watermelons long and round
When he plugs them
They make a juicy sound
Apples and oranges, plums and such
Squash and turnips
(I don't like them much)
We buy our market and he goes along
Singing his funny Araber song

       Mary Carter Smith
       ©1976

He who would eat of food must take his hand to it. (i.e. without working, one gets nothing to eat.)

An onion with a friend is a (roast) lamb.

The broth from a distance grows cool on the road.

It is the stinking bit of meat that catches the hyena.

African Proverbs

Akara

1 cup blackeye peas
fresh red pepper to taste (chopped)
1 medium sweet green pepper (cut into pieces)
½ teaspoon salt and seasonings of your choice
⅓ cup cold water
1 small onion (chopped)

DIRECTIONS:
Pick and wash blackeye peas. Cover them with water and let them set overnight. Drain water from peas. Use both hands to rub skins from peas. Again cover with water and skins will float to top. Drain water and skins. If necessary repeat process again until all skins are removed. Put peas in cold water. Let stand for 10-15 minutes to soften peas. Drain water. Place peas in blender and add the chopped onions, green pepper and red pepper. Blend to a paste. Put paste into a bowl and season to taste. Heat oil in frying pan. Form balls of paste with hands or spoon it into frying pan. Fry until browned evenly on all sides.

Mary Olandu From Nigeria

Baked Beans

4 large 53 oz. cans pork and beans
4 large onions chopped
Brown sugar, brown syrup or honey to taste (you may use all three or if you prefer use a brown sugar low calorie substitute)
3 tbs. spicy hot mustard
some bacon slices

DIRECTIONS:
Mix together the first four ingredients. Pour into greased pans. Bake uncovered for one hour at 375°. Lay slices of bacon on top beans. Cook for 15 minutes more.
Serves 20 people

Mary Carter Smith

Baked Potatoes in Blankets

1 lb. round steak, cut thin
5 medium baking potatoes
(about 2 lbs.)
⅓ cup flour
1 teaspoon salt
1 tablespoon fat

DIRECTIONS:
Pound the round steak with edge of heavy saucer or meat pounder and cut into pieces the proper size to wrap around the potatoes. Rub a small amount of salt on the pared raw potatoes and wrap the pieces of steak around them, fastening them with toothpicks. Roll in the flour mixed with salt and brown in hot fat. Place in a greased covered casserole, cover and bake in a moderately slow oven (325°) for 1 hour and 20 minutes or until potatoes are done. From time to time during the baking, pour on a small amount of hot water ot prevent drying of the steak. If desired, catsup may be put over the meat a few minutes before serving, and if any liquid remains in the bottom of the casserole it may be served as gravy.
5 servings.

Alice McGill

Beans – White, Boiled, Vegetarian

1 lb. Navy beans
1 tablespoon salt
6 cups water
2 medium onions, chopped
1 28 oz. can tomatoes or several fresh tomatoes cut into pieces
salt and black pepper to taste

DIRECTIONS:
Pick and wash beans. Soak overnight in cold water and salt. Next morning add two cups cold water to beans. Cover pot. Place over low flame and boil for 2½ hours. Add tomatoes, onions, salt and pepper. Continue cooking until beans are tender. If more water is needed while beans are cooking be sure to add only hot water.

VARIATION:
You may cook beans with ham, left-over ham bones and meat, pieces of slab bacon or smoked neckbones if you prefer to have meat.
Serves six people

Mary Carter Smith

Boiled Carrots

2 bunches carrots, sliced lengthwise
½ cup sugar
¾ stick butter (6 tablespoons)
salt and pepper to taste
One large bay leaf

DIRECTIONS:
Clean and slice carrots. Place carrots in enough water to cover them in the pot. Bring water to rolling boil; cover and cook over **Low Heat**.

Let simmer for 2 hours, water will boil down. During last half hour, add sugar and 3 tablespoons butter, continue cooking over **Low Heat**.

Remove bay leaf. Serve hot with 3 tablespoons butter atop carrots.
Serves 4-6. Preparation time: Approximately 2½ hours.

Margaret Williams

Candied Sweets

2 lbs. sweet potatoes – orange – colored
(if you can't find them, yellow ones will do.)
4 cups sugar
1 orange and/or lemon, **skins on**
1 stick of butter
1 teaspoon cinammon
½ teaspoon nutmeg

DIRECTIONS:
Peel potatoes and cut into desired serving size. Wash them and put in pot of cold water to cover. Boil potatoes slowly for 20-25 minutes. Pour off most of the water. Add sugar, orange or lemon pieces, butter, cinammon, nutmeg. Cook uncovered over low flame until sweet potatoes and fruit are candied. The syrup will be clear and juicy. Keep syrup to re-warm any leftovers. The fruit will be quite tasty. Enjoy the whole dish.

Recipe – Mary Day Nowden, my grandmother
M.C.S.

Coleslaw with Tomatoes

1 head medium green cabbage, slivered
1 large green pepper, cut into strips
2 medium-sized Spanish onions, cut into rings
1 cup sugar
2 tsp. sugar
1 tsp. dry mustard
1 tsp. celery seed
1 table. salt
1 cup vinegar
¾ cup salad oil
1 cup cherry tomatoes, halved.

DIRECTIONS:

In large bowl make layers of cabbage, green pepper, and onion, sprinkle 1 cup sugar over top.

In saucepan combine mustard, 2 tea. sugar, celery seed, salt, vinegar and oil. Mix well. Bring to a full boil, stirring. Pour over coleslaw. Refrigerate covered, at least 4 hours to serve, add tomatoes, toss salad to mix well. (8 servings)

COMMENTARY:

This I first tasted at a Storytelling Retreat at a beautiful, quiet place called Kirkridge, in the Poconos of Pennsylvania. I do not know the lady's name who gave me this recipe.

Mary Carter Smith

Corn Pudding

1 can Pet milk
3 eggs
½ to ¾ cup sugar
1 teaspoon vanilla
1 teaspoon nutmeg
2 tablespoons flour or cornstarch
1 can crushed (creamed) corn
1 can whole kernel corn, drained
½ to 1 stick butter or margarine, melted

DIRECTIONS:
Combine milk, eggs, sugar, salt, vanilla, nutmeg and flour. Beat well at medium speed until light and fluffy. Add both kinds of corn; REMEMBER - Drain the whole kernel corn! Add melted butter; stir well.

Pour mixture into greased dish or pan. HINT: Stir mixture again just before placing in oven.

Bake at 350° for 45 minutes. Top should be browned slightly. Pudding is done if a knife is clean after insertion in cooked food.

Margaret C. Turner

COMMENTARY:
Margaret is a whiz at producing this delicious dish. She graciously consented when I asked to share the recipe. It is a favorite among her guests and friends.

E.M.W.

SPECIAL NOTE:
The Lawson family recipe for corn pudding is similar to Margaret's, but the differences intrigued me. I think you'll be intrigued too. The differences are essentially in the ingredients; such as:

4 large or 6 small eggs
1 large can Pet milk
2 cups sugar
3 cans of corn - 1 creamed, 2 whole kernel (white or yellow)*
1 stick of margarine (softened to room temp.)

*Priscilla Lawson Marshall (my source) recommends shoe peg corn; she says it makes a better pudding!

E.M.W.

Crisp String Beans

1 pound fresh string beans
1 small onion, chopped
1 clove garlic chopped
¼ tea salt
½ stick softened margarine
½ tsp. marjoram
⅛ tsp. savory
½ tsp. basil
½ tsp. chervil
¼ cup sunflower seeds
1 tsp. chopped parsley
1 tsp. chopped chives
⅛ tsp. thyme
salt and pepper to taste

DIRECTIONS:
Take ends from green (string) beans. Remove strings. Cut or break into pieces. Wash string beans. Pour ½ cup water into heavy frying pan. Add salt. Put over medium flame and allow to come to boiling point. Lower flame. Add onions and garlic. Cook for one minute. Add beans. Cover and cook for fifteen minutes. Pour off liquid. In small bowl mix margarine, spices, and herbs. Stir until margarine is melted. Add to vegetables in frying pan. Then add sunflower seeds, salt, and pepper. Cover and cook for one minute. Serve hot. Serves four people.

Joyce Robertson

COMMENTARY:
Mrs. Robertson has become an expert in natural cooking. She agreed to use a little salt and pepper when the taste was a little too flat for most people. Some of us who have tried this recipe prefer to cook the string beans a little longer than in this recipe.

M.C.S.

Feijoado
(Black beans)

2 lbs. black beans (soaked)
½ lb. diced salt pork
½ lb. diced sausage
1 or 2 ham hocks
1 bay leaf
½ cup olive or vegetable oil
1 medium sized onion (chopped)
2 medium sized tomatoes (chopped)
2 cloves
dash of minced garlic (garlic powder may be used)
1 tsp. salt
½ tsp. pepper
¼ tsp. crushed hot red peppers
1 to 2 tbsp. dried parsley flakes

DIRECTIONS:
For the unusual Feijoada, soak two pounds of black beans overnight in water. Drain, cover with fresh water then add diced salt pork, sausage, ham hocks or pork shoulder chops and bay leaf. Bring to a boil, lower heat and simmer about 2 hours, or until beans are almost done. Meanwhile, heat olive or vegetable oil in skillet. Add onion, tomatoes, cloves, and garlic. Cook until vegetables are tender. Stir in salt, pepper, crushed hot red peppers and parsley flakes. Add 1 cup cooked beans and mash thoroughly. Stir vegetable mixture into meat and beans and continue to cook until mixture thickens. Accompany with white rice, greens or orange slices. Serves 10-12

COMMENTARY:
Although this dish comes from Brazil, it has African roots, reportedly being brought to Brazil by Africans. Hot and Wonderful!

Mary Carter Smith

Fried Green Tomatoes

6 medium-sized green tomatoes
½ tea salt
¼ tea black pepper
1 cup corn meal
¼ cup oil (vegetable or bacon drippings) *

DIRECTIONS:
Wash tomatoes. Cut off stems. Slice fairly thick. In paper bag mix corn meal, salt and pepper. Shake. Put sliced tomatoes in bag until slices are coated. Heat oil in heavy frying pan. Lay slices of tomatoes in hot oil and fry until brown on each side. Serve while hot.
Serves two people

* Amount of oil may vary depending if you like your food cooked in deep fat or not.

                                                            Mary Carter Smith

Fried Okra, Corn and Tomatoes

1 lb. fresh tender okra
2 large ears of corn
3 medium fresh tomatoes (1 lb.)
1 teaspoon salt
½ teaspoon black pepper
½ cup corn meal
¾ cup vegetable oil

DIRECTIONS:
Wash okra. Cut tips and stems off okra. Cut okra into slices about ¼ inch thick. Shuck and silk corn then cut corn off the cob. Wash and cut tomatoes into pieces. Put okra, corn kernals and tomatoes in a bowl. Add salt, black pepper and corn meal. Put vegetable oil into a frying pan and heat pan to a high temperature. Slide ingredients from bowl into hot oil. Place top on pan for a few minutes. This dish needs tender, loving care. Stir and turn often so ingredients do not stick to the pan. Cook until vegetables are done. If you like your vegetables crisp, cooking time will be shorter. Cook to your taste.

Recipe - Aunt Booby
Willie Nowden McAdory
M.C.S.

Greens

Collards
Turnip tops
Fat back, slab bacon, ham hocks, ham pieces
Salt
Dried red peppers

DIRECTIONS:
Pick your turnips or collards by taking off large stems on ends, checking to be sure there are no insects, weeds, etc., on greens. Wash greens thoroughly. Often turnip greens contain sand, so be sure to wash them well. I wipe collard leaves with a paper towel, then roll several leaves together and cut into strips before I wash them. I cook turnip greens with the leaves whole. For one pound of either green I use a piece of fat back or slab bacon about four inches square. Whatever meat I use, I boil the meat until it is just done before adding my greens. Season with salt to taste. I buy hot peppers at the Farmer's Market and string them to last throughout the year. Add only about ¼ of a pod unless you like your greens highly seasoned.

COMMENTARY:
While I named collards and turnip tops, these general directions can be followed with beet tops, sweet potato tops (a favorite in Africa), mustard greens or kale. Also you may peel turnip bottoms, cut into large pieces and cook with the tops.

Mary Carter Smith

A sister invited a brother home after church. They sat in the kitchen where the sister was stirring a pot of greens she was warming for dinner. The dear sister had a cold, and she was sniffling. She asked, "Brother Jones won't you stay for dinner?" Observing how she was sniffling, he replied, "Depending upon how the drop falls."

Greens In Chicken Broth

One four-pound stewing chicken, whole
1 tsp salt
Four pounds of greens (collards, kale, turnips, etc.)
Salt and black pepper to taste
Two tbsp sugar
1 tbsp chicken base (found at specialty stores) or
3 chicken bouillon cubes

DIRECTIONS:
Clean and wash whole stewing chicken well. Put into large pot. Cover with cold water. Add tsp. salt. Cover pot. Place over low flame. Cook for 2½ hours until done. (Cooking time may vary depending on quality of chicken.) Take chicken out of broth. Pour some of broth off. It can be saved for seasoning other foods. Pick, cut if needed, and wash greens. Place in chicken broth. Add salt and pepper to taste. Add sugar. Add chicken base or bouillon cubes. Boil to desired tenderness. Slice pieces of chicken and lay on top of greens. Replace cover and heat before serving.

William Spencer

COMMENTARY:
Bill Spencer is a neighbor who is a caterer. He comes from North Carolina. Many people do not eat pork. This method gives greens flavor without using pork.

M.C.S.

Hoppin' John

1 cup blackeyed peas, dried
3 cups water
½ pound salt pork or bacon (ham hocks may also be used)
1 red pepper pod, crushed OR
1 teaspoon crushed red peppers
½ cup onions, chopped and sauteed
½ teaspoon garlic salt
1 teaspoon seasoned salt
3 cups cooked rice

DIRECTIONS:
Soak peas overnight in water to cover, OR cover peas with water and let stand 1 hour. Use this water to cook peas. Add seasoning meat (your choice) and crushed pepper and bring to a boil. Lower heat and simmer in covered pot until peas are tender, an hour or longer. Add sauteed onions and seasonings with rice to peas. Toss lightly.

Pour mixture into greased casserole dish and bake at 350° until liquid is absorbed and peas are heated through – about 30 minutes. Taste and season accordingly. Serve at once.
Serves 8-10

Charlotte Little

COMMENTARY:
See comment in recipe for chitterlings. If I hadn't found this recipe, we might not have had one for Hoppin' John. Mary wondered aloud about the scarcity of this recipe, so when I saw it, I kept it for inclusion here.

E.M.W.

from "The Town Mouse & the Country Mouse"
'Better beans in peace than cakes and ale in fear.'
by AESOP

Hot Vegetable Salad For One

3 mushrooms, sliced
1 stalk celery, chopped
¼ of a cucumber, chopped
a small slice of red cabbage, chopped
1 thin slice Spanish onion, chopped
¼ of a green pepper, chopped
3 large leaves of lettuce, torn
Celery and onion salt or powder and pepper to taste
1 slice of lite cheddar cheese, grated
3 slices bacon, fried and crumbled
1½ teaspoons olive oil
1 tablespoon Weight Watchers Mayonnaise or Lite Miracle Whip salad dressing
1 teaspoon mustard, prepared (Djon or French's)
Parsley flakes & India Relish (optional)

DIRECTIONS:
Fry bacon slowly as you prepare vegetables. Saute vegetables in olive oil over low heat. DO NOT COVER. When all vegetables are coated and tender, remove from heat. Let cool briefly. Make a bed of the lettuce. Add the vegetables. Sprinkle parsley flakes, celery and onion powder (salt, if allowed) and pepper over salad.

Add grated cheese and bacon crumbles. Top with mayonnaise and mustard. Put a dollop of India relish in center. Toss lightly and enjoy!
Serves 1

COMMENTARY:
I have sometimes increased this recipe to feed 2 or more people by simply adding more vegetables. The condiments and seasonings are added in the bowl. Everyone gets to choose and add his/her own spice.

Elmira M. Washington

Macaroni Salad

¾ cup mayonnaise or salad dressing
3 cups elbow macaroni or shells
2 teaspoons onion, grated
2 teaspoons salt
¼ teaspoon pepper
½ cup lima beans, cooked
½ cup peas, cooked
¼ cup pimento, chopped
¼ green pepper, chopped
¾ cup celery, chopped
2 eggs, hard boiled and chopped
1 medium can Tuna or 1 lb. shrimp, diced

DIRECTIONS:
Place mayonnaise or salad dressing in large salad bowl. Add remaining ingredients. Mix well (if dressing is thick, stir in a little milk.) Pack into mold of your choosing. Chill thoroughly. Unmold on serving plate. Garnish with salad greens, tomatoes, parsley or radishes.
Serves 12

COMMENTARY:
Use your favorite salad dressing when making this salad. Chicken may be substituted for the seafood; also turkey or even beef.

Elmira M. Washington

Marinated Cucumbers

2 large cucumbers, thinly sliced
½ Spanish onion, sliced for rings
½ cup white vinegar
1½ cups water
Pinch of sugar
2 tomatoes, sliced or chopped

DIRECTIONS:
Combine all ingredients except the tomatoes. Stir mixture gently and cover tightly. Chill thoroughly while mixture marinates; overnight is usually sufficient. Remove mixture from marinade to serve; add cut-up tomatoes to mixture.
Serves 8-10

Thelma Mason

COMMENTARY:
As I was selecting recipes from among the scraps of paper from every source you can imagine, I saw one that reminded me of Mama's cucumbers. So rather than use the printed one, I queried Mama about hers. She says the little pinch of sugar "brings something out of those cucumbers."

E.M.W.

Marinated Tomatoes

4 medium to large size tomatoes (firm)
1 bunch of scallions (green onions)
1 bottle Wishbone Herbed Seasoned Italian Dressing
dried basil, salt, & pepper

DIRECTIONS:
Cut tomatoes into slices at least ½ inch thick or less if you prefer. Place slices on a platter or in a shallow casserole. Chop scallions, include some of the tender green tops. Sprinkle chopped scallions over tomatoes. Lightly salt and pepper and sprinkle tomatoes/onions with dried basil leaves.

Drizzle Italian Herbed Seasoning Dressing lightly over tomatoes and onions. Place UNCOVERED in refrigerator for at least 4 hours. At serving time garnish with fresh parsley, ¼ cup hard boiled egg slices (optional). Serves 4

A. Katherine Gross

COMMENTARY:
I first tasted this recipe at club meeting. It looks just as good as it tastes. Kitty doesn't take credit for the origin of the recipe, but she has admitted to "fiddlin" with it.

E.M.W.

Mushrooms And Scallions

10-12 large mushrooms, sliced
2-3 scallions (green onions), chopped
⅛ teaspoon celery salt
⅛ teaspoon pepper
2 tablespoons margarine, melted

DIRECTIONS:
Melt the margarine; season with celery salt. Add the scallions and saute lightly over LOW HEAT. Add mushrooms; toss gently to coat evenly. Keep heat LOW! Cover and let simmer. Mushrooms will produce their own juice. Allow mixture to SIMMER for 10-15 minutes. Stir occasionally until mushrooms are light brown and tender. Salt and pepper to taste. Serve immediately.
Serves 4

COMMENTARY:
Mushrooms "cook down", so don't be misled and skimp because you start with a panful. They will shrink as they cook. This recipe makes a great side dish and is a low-calorie vegetable.

Elmira M. Washington

Mushrooms In Cheese Sauce

1 lb. mushrooms
½ cup sour cream
2 dashes of pepper
1 tablespoon parsley flakes
½ cup cheddar cheese, grated
4 tablespoons butter
Dash of salt
1 tablespoon flour

DIRECTIONS:
Clean and slice mushrooms. Melt butter in skillet (Add celery salt or powder and ¼ tsp. Accent if desired.) Saute mushrooms until lightly browned. Remove from stove and add to mushrooms: sour cream, salt, pepper and flour. Transfer mixture to a buttered baking dish. Sprinkle parsley flakes and cheese over top. Bake at 350° from 20 to 25 minutes.

TIPS FOR MUSHROOMS
This recipe can be increased, but with careful measuring. All ingredients should be increased by half. Seasonings are added to taste and special care is taken with sour cream and butter. Sour cream and butter should only be increased by ¼ to prevent mixture from being too juicy. Choose a baking dish that will accommodate the amount of mushrooms used.
Preparation time: Approximately 45 minutes
Serves 6

COMMENTARY:
I have used this recipe many times and my guests ALWAYS want it. It is probably floating all over Baltimore by now. I've included it so that all of our friends can have it on hand for dinners or parties. It will always be a hit.

                                                            Elmira Washington

Okra Stew

1 lb. okra
2 medium onions
2 peppers
Palm oil or peanut oil
1½ lbs. meat or fish
Salt to taste

DIRECTIONS:
Wash okra in water. Put in a dish or platter for the water to dry out. Then cut the top and ends off. Slice into small pieces. Chop onions and peppers. Put oil in frying pan. When the oil is hot add okra. Let it fry until the slime is out. Add onions, peppers, meat or fish and a half cup of water. Let it stew down.

Liberia
Mary Carter Smith

Poke Salad

15 stalks young poke salad
1 bunch spring onions (6-8)
1 tbsp. bacon drippings or margarine
Salt and pepper to taste

DIRECTIONS:
Use only leaves and tender stalks. Wash. Place in pot. Cover with cold water. Parboil for ten minutes. Drain water. Wash and chop spring onions. In heavy fryer place bacon drippings or margarine. When oil is hot place drained poke salad and onions in frying pan. Add salt and pepper to taste. Cook until tender. (I only cook mine for about five minutes.)

COMMENTARY:
When we lived in West Virginia we enjoyed going to pick wild greens, such as poke salad, dandelion, etc. Poke salad is my favorite. Now it can be found in Spring at Farmer's Market, or growing, even in backyards in the city.

Mary Carter Smith

Potato Salad

2 lbs. white potatoes
1 tablespoon salt
3 stalks celery chopped
2 medium onions chopped
6 tablespoons fat
3 hard-boiled eggs
hot sauce to taste
½ teaspoon garlic powder
1 tablespoon sugar
1 tablespoon spicy hot mustard
1 tablespoon vinegar
Mayonnaise to taste

DIRECTIONS:
Peel, wash and dice potatoes. Add 1 tablespoon salt to water and cook until just done. Meanwhile, put fat into a frying pan. Add celery and onion to oil and saute over a low flame. Stir often. Next drain potatoes in a colander. Place in bowl and add sauteed vegetables, chopped eggs, hot sauce, garlic powder, sugar, vinegar, mustard and mayonnaise.
Serves 6 people

Mary Carter Smith

Ratatouille With Mushrooms

1 medium eggplant, peeled and cut in chunks
2 large zucchinis, cut in 1 inch chunks
2 large onions, sliced for rings
2 medium green peppers, julienne sliced
1 garlic clove, minced
1 large can tomatoes, sliced OR 4 medium-sized tomatoes, sliced
1 cup mushrooms, sliced
¼ cup olive oil
Seasonings: salt, pepper, curry powder, Italian seasoning, basil, rosemary, oregano.

DIRECTIONS:
Use a large skillet or pot. Heat oil over medium heat; add onions and garlic. Saute lightly. Add all other ingredients and seasonings to your taste. Stir to mix well. Cover; lower heat to the point where food will simmer, not boil! Stir occasionally so vegetables will not stick. Cook for about ½ hour. Remove cover; let simmer about 15 minutes so fluids will thicken.

Ground beef or chicken may be added to this recipe to make a one dish dinner. If ground beef is used, brown it first, then add the meat halfway through the cooking time.

If chicken is used, skin it so the fluid will not be too oily; add chicken along with the vegetables to give it sufficient time to be thoroughly cooked.

Doris Waters

COMMENTARY:
This is a highly versatile dish. It can be used as a main dish or a side dish; Doris suggests adding macaroni or rice if a starch is desired in the mixture. The mixture can be served over rice or macaroni too. It is a low calorie recipe.

E.M.W.

Sauerkraut

1 lb. pig tails, spare ribs or neck bones
1 quart sauerkraut
Salt and pepper to taste
2 lettuce leaves
½ tart apple
celery leaves
1 tablespoon vinegar
4-6 white potatoes, cut in fourths (optional)

DIRECTIONS:
Cook the meat about half-done. Season to taste. Add sauerkraut, place lettuce leaves in center. Put apple into center of lettuce. Add celery leaves and vinegar. Cook over medium heat for 1½ to 2 hours. Add hot water if necessary. During last ½ hour, add potatoes.
Serves 4

Lola W. Taylor

COMMENTARY:
If possible, cook this recipe and let the kraut set over-night. It always tastes better the next day.

You can substitute apple sauce, a big spoonful, if you don't have an apple. When I cook sauerkraut, I dump everything in the pot together, add a lump of butter and let it all "stew" for a few hours. Delicious!

E.M.W.

7 Layer Salad

1 head lettuce, shredded (and/or) raw spinach, shredded
2 green peppers, chopped
1 cup Spanish onions, chopped
1 cup celery, chopped
*1 pkg. frozen baby peas
1 can water chestnuts (optional), sliced
1 pint mayonnaise
2 tablespoons sugar
4-6 oz. cheddar cheese
8 strips bacon, fried and crumbled

DIRECTIONS:
Place a layer of each vegetable in a large salad bowl. DO NOT MIX *Peas may be cooked and drained.
1. Mix sugar, bacon and mayonnaise. Spread over top layer, then sprinkle cheese. Cover well with cheese.
OR
2. Make a hole in middle after layers are placed in bowl. Put mayonnaise mixture in the hole. Cover and refrigerate for 8 hours or over-night. Toss just before serving. Garnish (optional)

NOTE:
The vegetables can vary. Others that may be added include radishes, carrots, mushrooms, cherry tomatoes.
Serves 15-20
Compilation of 2 recipes

Joan Kraft
Vanessa McCoy Simms

COMMENTARY:

We found at least 4 versions of this beautiful salad; we compiled 2 of them for our own version.

Mrs. Simms cautions, "If you add cherry tomatoes, don't cut them. They're too wet. They'll soggy up your spinach. Throw them in whole."

NOTE OF INTEREST
The 4th recipe included potatoes, none of the others did.

E.M.W.

Stringbeans, Carrots And Onions

1 pound stringbeans, sliced
4 med. carrots, sliced lengthwise and cut in half
1 very large onion OR 2 medium onions
1 tablespoon bacon drippings
Salt to taste
2 bay leaves, whole

DIRECTIONS:
Combine all veggies with bacon drippings in water to cover. Bring to boiling, then lower to medium heat and cook until the vegetables are tender as you like them. Serve hot; dot with thin pats of butter if desired.

Louise Gambrill

COMMENTARY:
This is one of those deceptive recipes that tastes so good after the cooking is done, that you wonder why you didn't think of it yourself.

E.M.W.

Stuffed Baked Potatoes

8 large potatoes, baked
3 cups cheddar cheese, (sharp natural) shredded.
½ cup salad dressing
¼ cup milk
2 eggs
½ teaspoon salt
Dash of pepper
½ cup scallions, chopped (green onions)
8 bacon slices, cooked & crumbled

DIRECTIONS:
Cutting lengthwise, remove a slice from the top of each potato; OR cut each potato in half, lengthwise. Scoop out potato; leave a ⅛ inch shell. Combine potato with 2 cups cheese, eggs, salad dressing, milk and seasonings; beat well. Mixture should be fluffy and light. Fill the potato shells; top with rest of cheese, onions and bacon. Bake in 350° oven for about 15 minutes or until tops of potatoes are golden brown.
Serves 8 or 16

COMMENTARY:
One of my favorite foods is baked potatoes. I began to experiment with ways to "jazz" them up a little. One of the ways I used was to scoop out the middle and add things to the potato, then bake the mixture. Imagine how happy I was to find a similar recipe. I just combined the two; that's why the cutting part has a dual entry. Of course you can change the ingredients to suit yourself.

Elmira Washington

Stuffed Cabbage Rolls

1 small head of cabbage
1 lb. ground beef
2 teaspoons chopped onion
1 egg, beaten
½ cup milk
1 teaspoon salt

DIRECTIONS:
Trim off soiled leaves of cabbage and remove core. Cover with boiling water and let stand 5 minutes or until cabbage leaves are limp. Separate leaves carefully reserving five of the largest leaves for the rolls. Combine meat thoroughly with onion, egg, milk, and salt. Place 1/5 of the meat mixture on each leaf and fold up envelope fashion. Fasten with tooth pick. Lay flap down, in Dutch oven or saucepan. Add ½ cup water, and cover rolls with rest of cabbage leaves.

Simmer, covered, for 1 hour. Serve with tomato sauce.
Serves 5

Alice McGill

Vegetable Medley

12 med. mushrooms, sliced
½ medium sized cabbage, chopped
1 green pepper, chopped
1 sweet red pepper, chopped
3 stalks crisp celery, chopped
1 medium Spanish onion, sliced for rings
4 scallions, chopped
1 large cucumber, sliced
1 large zucchini, sliced
2 medium cans sliced tomatoes, or 2 firm tomatoes sliced thinly
12 slices bacon, fried and crumbled (optional)
Salt and pepper to taste
Celery and garlic salt or powder may be used.
2 tablespoons fresh parsley
1 tablespoon thyme
1 tablespoon dry mustard
1 teaspoon Worcestershire sauce
2 bay leaves
2 tablespoons olive oil

DIRECTIONS:
Clean and prepare vegetables: set aside. Pour olive oil into fry pan or dutch oven over medium heat until warm. Combine all seasonings and vegetables **EXCEPT** zucchini, cucumbers and tomatoes. Over low heat, mix vegetables until all are coated; work slowly and gently. Saute slowly until vegetables are tender but still crispy - about 10 minutes. Cover, let simmer **slowly** for about 5 minutes. Turn off heat.

Remove bay leaves. Add zucchini and cucumber slices, gently mixing among other vegetables. Cover and saute over low heat for 5 minutes or until zucchini and cukes are tender. Drain canned tomatoes and pour over entire mixture during last 3 or 4 minutes. If using fresh tomatoes, add after zucchini and cucumbers.

Bacon crumbles may be sprinkled over the vegetables just before serving. Drain bacon on paper towels before crumbling. Serve immediately.
Preparation Time: Approximately 25-40 minutes.
Serves 10

Lola W. Taylor

COMMENTARY:
I watched Lola concoct this recipe one day a couple of years ago. The first chance I got, I served it at a dinner party. Well! I've been giving out Lola's creation ever since. She was surprised that I'd picked up all of the steps she used; she was also happy that I didn't lay claim to the credit. I couldn't do that to Lo!

E.M.W.

Yellow Squash Souffle

Preheat Oven to 350°
3 tbsp. butter
1 cup cracker crumbs
1 lb. cooked squash, chopped
2 onions, chopped
2 eggs, beaten
½ cup grated cheese
Salt and pepper to taste
1 cup milk

DIRECTIONS:
Melt butter in hot milk, pour over craker crumbs. Mix together squash, seasonings, onion, eggs and ½ cup of cracker crumbs, in a greased baking dish.

Top with ½ cup cracker crumbs and cheese. Bake at 350° for 30 minutes.
Preparation time: Approximately 45 minutes.
Serves 6

Mozella Blackwell

The Stories

"I cannot imagine life without books. Reading is my escape; I can be anyone, go everywhere, do anything at anytime in the past, the present or the future. Reading teaches me, entertains me, informs me, enlarges my world, keeps me humble and satisfies my curiosity."

Elmira M. Washington

The Last Shot

Alice McGill

She saw the two of them walking down the long, narrow lane leading to the house. Instantly, she stopped the porch swing where she had been pumping herself back and forth. She gazed in the distance. If they had had a car it was parked on the road way up beyond the grove of pine trees. Their two dark skirts swayed in unison as they walked, purposely putting one foot before the other in the soft dirt. They were the first visitors in a long time, save the two men who brought big spray guns and sprayed the house, barn and pig pen. The sun's heat waves rippled in front of the two women and distorted the outlines of their bodies. Each of them was carrying a black case. She began to count their steps and tap the rhythm of their bodies.

"Go in the house and tell Ma, somebody comin'," said an urgent voice.

She almost fell off the porch swing as she turned quickly to face the voice of her older brother, Bo Jack. Beads of perspiration stood out like blisters on his forehead. He had come around the house from the back field she supposed.

"You go tell her your ownself," she whined and turned to face the two who kept walking and who, now seemed to be talking to each other. She could tell by the way they looked at each other every now and then. She wondered about the subject of their conversation. She wondered if they were nice like the "lot of people" who had come and brought steaming pots and bowls of food ... potato pies and ...

"Go in the house, Dottie!" Her brother screamed a whisper with his lips ironed against clenched teeth.

She jumped off the swing and walked slowly toward the front door. She looked back at Bo Jack so that he could see her roll her eyes and suck her teeth at him. But his thirteen-year-old body had assumed an air of nonchalance as he slumped in the swing.

The front door opened easily into a wide hallway. On one side of the hall was the kitchen and on the other, two bedrooms. The back door was at the other end of the hall. A typical "shot gun" house folks used to laugh and say. "You can shoot from the front to the back and never hit a thing." The inside was surprisingly cool. She sucked in the pleasant cross breeze created by the open kitchen and bedroom windows.

"Ma, here come somebody," she said softly to her mother's back.

Madry Epps didn't look up from her quilting frame. A fence rail pattern hung from the ceiling and spread out before her like welcoming hands.

"Who is it?" She asked.

"I don't know. They almos' to the house."

Her mother eased her body from under the quilting frame and smiled at her five-year-old daughter. The fresh white washed walls contrasted their rich brown skins.

"Lemme see who it it. Be Ma's little lady, now and go call Bo Jack for me."

"He already out there." The little smile that played at the corners of her mother's mouth made her feel glad that she had come to announce the approaching visitors. I think they got suitcases and all, and it's two of 'em - they dressed just alike, too."

"Ain't that nice," her mother replied.

The woman turned to the opposite wall and straightened the old Walker's Almanac calendar. It seemed that a long time passed before the eight-day clock invaded the quiet with its two loud gongs. The child detected the almost inaudible sigh in her mother's shoulders . . . now she was walking briskly to the front door.

"Hi do!" Her mother was speaking in a singing voice.

Dottie peeped around her mother's skirt. Instantly she was riveted to a pair of strange eyes ... eyes that reminded her of her cat. Their navy blue dresses showed skinny waists.

"Well, how're you doing today, Madry?" one of them spoke happily.

"We comin' along fine I thank you, Miss Maude."

"Well, Madry," the shorter and older one intoned. "I want to introduce Mrs. Alsbrook, here, to you. She's in training with me. You know Mrs. Simmons retired from public health nursing three weeks ago, and Mrs. Alsbrook is taking her place."

Her mother nodded and continued to stand as if she was trying to block the door way. The two white women flashed their eyes around the porch as if to survey the unpainted clapboard and the rough hewn surface of the porch floor. They focused on Bo Jack who was wiping his brow with the back of his hand. The one whom her mother called "Miss Maude" began to talk at Bo Jack.

"My goodness, he's growing so nice and strong. I bet you're a great help to your mother, aren't you, James Edward? How old are you now?"

"Goin' on fourteen and everybody call me, Bo Jack."

"Have you had any fever since the last time I was here?"

"No."

"That's good, but I'm going to have to take your temperature anyway."

"Her fingers must have done something," the child thought. She heard a bong sound and the case flipped up by itself. She took a small step forward to examine the shiny fixings on the black case.

"After I take your temperature, I'll give you your last shot." The nurse's last three words triggered something in the child's memory. She did not know what to think. Maybe it was the way the words were said, or was it the straw colored hair, or the raw-looking skin that was sprinkled with brown spots. The three words whirled in her head and she searched to place them in another time.

The Last Shot

Miss Maude's sharp voice spoke directly to the younger nurse.

"This family was one of the hardest hit in Samee County when the fever epidemic broke out in May. Three family members didn't survive ... the father, Daniel Epps, age thirty-eight; two siblings, Eunice, age seventeen, and Junius, age eight."

"We are taking precautions by giving injections to the survivors."

"Ma!" Bo Jack screamed in pain and leaped the short distance to their mother's side. Madry Epps was slowly sinking to the floor. He grabbed her arm but could do no more than break her fall as she came to rest against the door jam. "Ma, Ma ..." Bo Jack pleaded.

The two nurses rushed to help. Bo Jack blocked their path.

"You didn't have no business comin' here talkin' 'bout it."

"All you had to do was give us our last shots and go on to somebody else's house."

There it was again ... "last shot." No one noticed as she backed her small body into the hallway corner and sat down. "Last shot ... last shot – " The words came to her in another voice and time ... Junius's voice, laughing and showing her how to shoot marbles.

"Sicker first!" Junius pounced at her from the China berry tree. She knew "sicker first," was a signal to shoot marbles and that Junius was going to be first. She watched him etch a triangle in the dirt with a piece of broken glass. He skillfully dropped a marble on each corner of the triangle. Then, he placed seven or eight marbles inside the triangle.

"I'm rolling 'Big Steel,' you can roll 'Big Aggie,'" he said, and pressed an oversized marble in her out stretched hand. She studied the swirling blue and yellow colors.

"You got to watch me," he warned. "I'm gonna stand 'bout this far back from them marbles and roll like this." He stood as still as he could like he was thinking real hard. He let go an underhand toss. The sun's light picked up the glint in the steel ball as it bounced over the hard earth. She remembered when her Pa brought two steel balls home from the peanut factory. They were the same size as "Big Aggie," but heavier.

"Look at him go!" Junius shouted.

Her eyes followed "Big Steel" as it rolled through the triangle and knocked out three marbles.

"Now, they belong to me 'cause I knocked them out of the triangle." Junius was talking fast. "It's my turn again until I don't knock any more marbles out."

He crouched on his knees where "Big Steel" had stopped rolling and tucked the ball in the crook of his thumb and forefinger. His thumb propelled the shiny ball toward the triangle. It missed its mark and came to a standstill on the other side of the triangle. "Now it's your turn," Junius directed. "Move back just a little bit more."

The Last Shot

She tossed "Big Aggie" through the triangle, and knocked out one marble.

"That's good!" Junius praised her.

"I know it's good," she bragged.

He laughed. "I'm gonna knock them all out the next time, so go 'head and shoot' cause this gonna be your last shot ... your last shot ... your last shot ..." His image whirled away from her.

"Dottie, com' on, get up baby." Her mother's soothing tones worked their way into her head. You worried 'bout Ma. She alright. Just had a little ol' weak spell that's all. Stop it, now."

She felt herself being picked up, but she didn't know what to stop until Bo Jack wiped a cloth across her face. Then she heard herself sobbing. When she sealed her lips to stop the sobs, mournful sighs came through her nose. When she opened her mouth to speak, more sobs twisted her body back and forth. She wanted to tell about Junius and "Big Steel" and "Big Aggie," but she didn't know how.

"Madry, I'm so sorry," murmured Miss Maude. "I didn't know that ... well I wish I ..."

Don' worry, Miss Maude," her mother interrupted.

Through her blur of tears she saw the two nurses staring down over her mother's shoulder. Miss Maude had a look of far away pity pasted across her face. Mrs. Alsbrook kept blinking her eyes as if a piece of trash had blown in them.

Madry stood and held her child close. Words began to flow out of her mouth. The woman spoke to no one in particular.

"Seem like it all come down on me at once, but we gonna be alright, now. I feel it. This baby showed me what was wrong."

"See, I ain't been talking 'bout it. I lost my mate and my two children and I ain't never cried 'bout it either 'cause I thought I had to be strong for the two I got left."

"Madry, maybe it'd be best if we ..." Miss Maude started.

"You know what, Miss Maude!" her mother shouted. "Keeping a dry eye ain't got nothin' in the world to do with strength."

Dottie felt the movement of her mother's body as the words kept flowing. The child closed her eyes and drew comfort from the heaving chest.

"I'm gonna talk 'bout my husband, Daniel and my daughter, Eunice, and my son, Junius. I'm gonna listen to Dottie and Bo Jack talk about them, too. I'm gonna rip up that quilting frame and I'm gonna cry whenever I feel like it."

Dottie tightened her arms around her mother's neck; She felt her mother's tears dropping on her shoulder. Bo Jack came into her view as her mother paced the floor. Tears were streaming down his face, too. He was smiling.

Mrs. Alsbrook cleared her throat two or three times before she finally spoke. "Well, when Miss Maude told me we were visiting here today I put something special in my bag for Dottie and Bo Jack. So, after we give you the last shots I'll bring the special things out."

"What is it?" Dottie scrambled down out of her mother's arms. "Can I see it?"

Mrs. Alsbrook smiled at Dottie and reached to shake the hand of Madry Epps. "I want to say to you, Mrs. Epps, I'm proud to be serving your family."

"Thank you, M'am," her mother smiled. The smile was true.

Miss Maude looked at the younger nurse as if she had done a "terrible wrong." Her lips became thin pink lines.

"Come on out to the porch." The younger nurse's face changed to a deep pink as she glanced at Miss Maude. "Well, we have to get this show on the road," she chimed. "Do you want to be first, Bo Jack?"

"Yes, M'am!" Bo Jack almost shouted.

"How 'bout the special thing in your bag for us?" Dottie wedged. She had to speak quickly or they would start talking to each other again.

"I said after your last shot," teased Mrs. Alsbrook.

Notes on Cindy Ellie

CINDY ELLIE is an original story that began as part of a routine I present, on occasion, as a tribute to Jackie "Moms" Mabley. For "Moms" was a grand lady. Between her guffaws of laughter there were strong messages of social and racial justice. This story is placing the traditional Cinderella in the urban setting of my adopted home, Baltimore City. Although it is protected by copyright (1982) I will give permission for other storytellers to use it if I am asked and credited. CINDY ELLIE can be adapted for use in any city.

The oral narration preceded the written story. It is written in a mixture of street, average, and traditional English. I am pleased with the popularity it has attracted. CINDY ELLIE is high on the lists of requests when I perform.

Parts of CINDY ELLIE were recorded from a live performance at the tenth anniversary of NAPPS (National Association for the Preservation and Perpetuation of Storytelling) in Jonesborough, Tennessee in 1982. This is part of the film BY WORD OF MOUTH. This film can be secured by writing to NAPPS, P.O. Box 112, Jonesborough, Tennessee, 37659. CINDY ELLIE is also presented as part of my 60-minute cassette tape MARY CARTER SMITH PRESENTS. This tape can be secured by writing to me at P.O. Box 11484, Baltimore, Maryland 21239.

It is advised to read this story with tongue in cheek. I only hope that some of the joy of creating, delivering, and writing CINDY ELLIE rubs off on you, the reader.

Mary Carter Smith

Cindy Ellie, A Modern Fairy Tale

Mary Carter Smith

    Once upon a time, over in East Baltimore, there lived a happy family: Sam Johnson, his wife, Lula, and their daughter, Ellie. Lula was good and kind; a quiet, church-going woman, but mighty puny and sickly. One day Lula called Ellie to her bedside. "Child, Mama ain't feeling so well. One of these days, I might leave you." "Oh, Mama, don't say that," Ellie said, with tears in her eyes. "Don't cry, child. All of us go sometime, and I'd rather it be me than you. So there are a few things I want to tell you. Always mind your daddy. Stay in church, go to school and learn that book. Remember what I'm telling you." "All right, Mama, I'll remember."
    One day, not long after, the poor woman just up and died; real peaceful-like and quiet.
    Honey, let me tell you, they had a beautiful funeral. Sam sure put her away nice. The Senior Choir turned out full force. The Junior Choir was there. And the Gospel Chorus just sung their hearts out! The church was CROWDED! Folks all on the outside, with loudspeakers going. Lula's lodge sisters was there in their white dresses, and them purple sashes all edged in gold. Ellie was on the front row beside her daddy. Just as cute as she could be in a white dress and her hair in a fine bush. Ellie was one purty young Black sister, her skin like Black velvet.
    Child, let me tell you, that poor woman's body wasn't hardly cold before them church sisters was after Sam Johnson, like flies after honey! 'Cause he had a good job down Sparrow's Point, with lots of seniority. And they had just paid for one of them pretty, big houses on Broadway, with them pretty white marble steps. It was a lovely block; won first prize in the AFRO Clean Block three years running!
    That poor man, like so many good men, was weak for a pretty face and big legs and big hips. One huzzy, the boldest of 'em all had a heart as hard as a rock. The milk of human kindness had curdled in her breast. But she did have a pretty face, big legs, and great big hips. Ooh-wee! She could put on! Made like she loved Ellie so, and was always bringing good barbecued ribs, collard greens, cracklin' bread, and jelly-layer cake to Ellie and Sam. Well that fool man fell right into that woman's trap. She had that man cornered and married before you could say, "Jackie Robinson."
    Then bless my soul. You ain't never seen such a change in nobody! First off that woman went down to Souse Car'lina for her two big-footed, ugly gals her Mama'd been keeping. Brought them back to Baltimore, and put poor Ellie out of her pretty room with the canopied bed and let her ugly gals sleep in that pretty room. Made poor little Ellie sleep on a pallet in the cellar.

Cindy Ellie, A Modern Fairy Tale

Now Ellie's mama had been wise. When everybody else was converting they furnaces to oil and gas, she said, "Uh-uh. One day they gone be hard to get." She had kept her coal furnace. Poor little Ellie had to do all the cooking, cleaning, washing and ironing. She had to scrub them marble steps twice a day and wait on them ugly gals hand and foot. Not only that, but in the winter she had to keep the fire going and clean out the ashes and cinders. So they got to calling her Cindy Ellie.

Tell you the truth, I believe that woman had put some roots on that man! 'Cause no matter how she mistreated Cindy Ellie, he never said a word, just CRAZY 'bout that big-legged woman.

That November, the good White folks, the good Asian folks, and the good Black folks all turned out and voted for a good Black brother, running for mayor. And he won the election by a landslide! He was having his inauguration ball down at the Convention Center. So many folks voted for him that they had to hold it for two nights running. The mayor's son had come home from college to go to the ball.

Oh, them stepsisters was primping and buying designer gowns to go to the ball. Poor Cindy Ellie had to give one a perm, the other a gerry curl and both of them facials; not that it helped much. Honey, them gals was ugly from the inside out!

"Cindy Ellie, don't you wish you could go to the ball?", they asked her.

"Oh, you are making fun of me" Cindy Ellie said.

So Cindy Ellie's daddy, her stepmother, and them two ugly gals all went to the ball and left poor Cindy Ellie home.

Now Cindy Ellie had a godma. She had been her dear mama's best friend, and she still had a key to the house. She came to the house, as she often did, to sneak food to poor Cindy Ellie and found the child laying on her hard pallet, just crying her heart out!

"Why are you crying, child?" she asked her.

"Be-because I want to go to the ball."

Now this godma had been born with a veil over her face, down in New Orleans. She knew a thing or two about voodoo and hoodoo. Besides that she had a High John the Conqueror Root, that she always used for good. The godma told Cindy Ellie, "Go upstairs to the kitchen, child. Look in the kitchen cabinet drawer and bring me the biggest white onion you can find. Cindy Ellie was an obedient child. She didn't ask, "Why?" She just did what her godma told her to do. Cindy Ellie brought her the onion. She gave it to her godma. Then they went out in the back yard. The godma laid that onion on the ground. Then she stepped back and waved that root over that onion! And right before their eyes that onion turned into a long white Cadillac that parked itself in the back alley!

"Cindy Ellie go up on the third floor and bring me that mouse trap." Cindy Ellie brought it down. There were two little black mice trapped in a little cage.

She told Cindy Ellie to open the door and them mice started out. But that godma waved that root over them and they turned into two six-foot tall Black chauffers dressed in shining white uniforms with fancy white caps! And they had on long black boots! And they was bowing and scraping. "All right, Cindy Ellie, you can go to the ball now."

"But, godma, look at me. I'm clean, but I'm ragged."

"Don't worry 'bout it," her godma said. Then she stepped back and waved that root over Cindy Ellie. Her rags turned into a dazzling dress of pink African laces! Her hair was braided into a hundred shining braids, and on the end of each braid were beads of pure gold! Her eyes were beautifully shaded and her skin was shining like polished ebony! Golden bracelets covered her arms clean up to her elbows! On each ear hung five small diamond earrings. On her tiny feet were dainty golden sandals encrusted with dazzling jewels! Cindy Ellie was laid back!

As one of the chauffers helped her into the white Cadillac her godma told her, "Be sure you leave before midnight or you'll be as you was. Your Cadillac will turn back into an onion, your chauffers into mice, and your clothes into rags." Cindy Ellie promised her godma that she would leave before midnight. Away she went, as happy as could be.

The mayor's son heard that a beautiful girl had arrived who looked like an African princess. He came out to see, and said to himself, "This sure is a fine fox!" He asked her, "May I escort you into the ballroom?" Cindy Ellie replied in tones soft and low, "I don't mind if you do." He helped her out of her limousine and escorted her into the ballroom and to the head table where he was sitting. Every eye was on Cindy Ellie. You could have heard a pin drop. Then voices could be heard, "Gorgeous," "Lovely," "Devastating," "Elegant," etc. etc. Even the mayor himself could not take his eyes off her. His wife agreed that she was indeed a charming young woman. The other ladies were looking at her clothes and wishing they had material in their gowns as beautiful as that in Cindy Ellie's.

Although the table was loaded with sumptuous food, Toussaint, the mayor's son couldn't eat a bite! Just busy looking at Cindy Ellie. In her honor, the band played the Ghanian High-Life. Cindy Ellie and Toussaint danced it as if they had been dancing together all their lives. Cindy Ellie was friendly and courteous to everyone she met. She even sat beside her stepsisters (who had no idea who she was) and invited them to come back the next night. For Toussaint had begged Cindy Ellie to return for the second night of the ball.

Then Cindy Ellie heard the clock strike, forty-five minutes after eleven! She murmered to Toussaint, "Really, I must be getting home." And she rushed out as fast as she could go.

As soon as she was home Cindy Ellie called her godma and thanked her for such a splendid time. The doorbell rang and she heard her stepsister's voices,

"Hurry, Stupid! Open the door!" Cindy Ellie came, yawning and rubbing her eyes, as if she'd been asleep. "Did you have a good time?" she asked. "Oh it was alright, but we didn't get to dance with the mayor's son. He danced only with some new girl. No one had seen her before. She had on some old African clothes. But on her they did look good. She did have the good sense to recognize what quality people we are and she had the mayor's son to invite all of us tomorrow night. "What was her name?" asked Cindy Ellie. "No one knows. The mayor's son is dying to find out who she is." Cindy Ellie said, "You don't mean it. Oh how I wish I could go to the ball tomorrow night. Lillie, won't you lend me your old blue gown so I can go also?" They almost split their sides laughing."You, with your ragged self going to the inauguration ball? Wouldn't that be something else! Of course not. Come and help us get undressed and turn back the covers on the bed, so we can go to sleep."

As on the night before poor little Cindy Ellie was left behind while the rest of them went to the ball again. Her godma came in and heard the child, crying again. "Why you crying, child? You want to go to that ball again?" "Yes, m'am." "I thought so. You've been a good child all your life and you always respect your elders. So don't worry. You can go to the ball again. Now dry your eyes and get your face together. Look in that kitchen cabinet drawer and bring me the biggest yellow onion you can find." Cindy Ellie came back with the biggest yellow onion you ever laid your eyes on. Then they went out in the back yard. The godma laid that onion on the ground. Then she stepped back and waved that root over that onion! And right before their eyes that onion turned into a solid gold Mercedes-Benz about half a block long! And it parked itself in the back alley.

"Cindy Ellie go up on the third floor and bring me that rat trap." Cindy Ellie brought it down. There were two big white rats trapped in a big wire cage.

That family lived so close to Johns Hopkins Hospital that mice and rats used to escape from them laboratories up there. They took that cage out in the back yard. She told Cindy Ellie to open the door and them rats started out. But that godma stood back and waved that High John the Conqueror root over them and they turned into two seven-foot tall White chauffers dressed in shining gold uniforms with fancy gold caps! And they had on shining white boots! And they was bowing and scraping.

"All right, Cindy Ellie, you can go to the ball now."

"But godma, look at me. I'm clean, but I'm ragged."

"Don't worry 'bout it" her godma said. Then she stepped back and waved that root over Cindy Ellie. Her rags turned into a dress made of pure silk kente, that royal cloth from Ghana! Worth thousands of dollars! On her head was a geelee of the rarest of taffeta, standing tall and stiff and just gorgeous! Her big pretty eyes were beautifully shaded and her skin was shining like polished ebony. Golden bracelets covered her arms clean up to her shoulders! On each ear hung five small diamond earrings. On her tiny feet were dainty golden sandals encrusted with dazzling jewels. She was cool!

As one of the chauffers helped her into that gold Mercedes-Benz her godma told her, "Be sure you leave before midnight or you'll be as you was. That Mercedes-Benz will turn back into an onion, your chauffers into rats, and your clothes into rags." Cindy Ellie promised her godma that she would leave before midnight. Away she went, as happy as could be.

As they drove up, Toussaint was waiting for her. She went into the ballroom draped on his arm. Oh they was having such a good time laughing and talking, and cha-cha-chaing, and waltzing, and boogeying! That poor child forgot all about time! Then she heard the clock as it began to strike twelve! She ran out of there as fast as her legs would carry her. She ran so fast, she ran out of one of those sandals. She put the other in her hand and ran on. Toussaint ran behind her, but he couldn't see where she had gone. He picked up the golden sandal.

He asked the security people, "Did you see an African princess run by you?" "No. We did see a girl dressed in rags run out of the door. We thought she had stole something. But that chick was gone!"

That night when the family came home from the ball they told Cindy Ellie, "Something mighty strange happened tonight. As the clock on City Hall began to strike twelve that African princess began to run like crazy! She ran so fast, she ran out of one of her golden sandals. The mayor's son found it and kept it. He just kept looking at it. He's really upset over that sister."

Child, the next day the mayor's son came on television, came on the radio, and announced to every paper in Baltimore that he would marry the girl whose foot would fit that sandal he had picked up. Now a lot of folks who had supported the mayor lived in the places surrounding Baltimore. So first all them sorority girls and debutantes, and folks like that, tried to fit their foot in that sandal. Wouldn't fit none of them girls in Columbia, Cockeysville, Randallstown and places like that. Then they went to them rich folk's houses up on Cadillac Row and places like that. Wouldn't fit none of them girls neither. Then they went to all them condominiums downtown by The Inner Harbor, and them fancy town houses. Wouldn't fit none of them neither. Finally they come to East Baltimore. Length and long they came to Broadway and knocked at the Johnson's residence. The mayor's men came in with that golden sandal on a red velvet pillow. Them two stepsisters tried their best to put on that shoe! They pushed, and they jugged. But their big feet would not get into that shoe. No way, Jose! "May I try?" asked Cindy Ellie. "No, Stupid. It's not for the likes of you." "Yes, you may try on the sandal," the mayor's representative said. "For the proclamation issued by the mayor said that any girl in Baltimore and surrounding areas may try. He spoke kindly to Cindy Ellie. "Sit down, miss and see if it fits you," And do you know, that sandal just slid on

Cindy Ellie, A Modern Fairy Tale

Cindy Ellie's little foot as smooth as silk. Then she pulled from the pocket in her clean but ragged dress the other sandal. As soon as she put it on her foot, right there before their very eyes, Cindy Ellie was transformed into the African princess they had seen the nights before! Them two stepsisters had a fit! "Oh Cindy Ellie, we didn't mean no harm! Oh Cindy Ellie, please forgive us!" They was on the floor rolling round and carrying on.

Cindy Ellie told them, "Get up off that floor and stop all that whooping and hollering. I forgive you."

Then Cindy Ellie was transported to the mayor's mansion in his private limousine. Toussaint was there waiting to welcome her with open arms. Cindy Ellie was true to her word. For she not only forgave her stepsisters in word but in deed. She found them two ugly councilmen for husbands. Toussaint and Cindy Ellie were married in the biggest Baptist church in East Baltimore and the reception was held in the Convention Center. And they lived happily, happily, forever after.

Mary Carter Smith

©1982

The Doberman's Dilemma

Elmira M. Washington

"Blast," she thought. "Light!"
Somehow light was penetrating her closed eyelids. She groaned in dismay and turned her back to the double windows.

"He left those shades up again," her brain recorded. Her husband's soft breathing continued undisturbed even when she deliberately bumped him as she rolled over.

They had both decided to leave the draperies open and take advantage of the cool breezes flowing from back to front in their small rowhouse. She assumed that he had decided to leave the shades halfway up for the same reason.

Daylight bounced off the butter-colored walls and ceiling and glowed over their double bed. He slept peacefully. She would never understand how the man could sleep with light shining right in his face.

"Never," she griped mentally. Keeping her eyes shut, she settled against his back and tried to match his steady breathing.

Sleep still evaded her though. Something besides light had disturbed her precious slumber.

She realized that she'd been ignoring the high-pitched insistent whining that now brought her to full wakefulness. The sound compounded the effect that the light had caused. She was unable to relax because her brain was busy concentrating on the site of the steady keening.

The crying was outside the house.

Her "mother's ear" recognized a summons in the wailing, but she could not identify the distressed creature. She was wide awake now.

Curiosity finished what light and sound had begun. She found herself sitting up in bed wondering why the cries didn't let up or change. She decided to investigate.

She took great care not to disturb her husband as she stole out of bed. That way she wouldn't have to explain. She grinned as she imagined him saying, "Will you for once just mind your own business. You can't do anything about whatever it is!" Then he'd probably insist and end up urging, "Come on back to bed. It's too early to be up anyway, Woman."

She tiptoed in triumph on bare feet across the cool hardwood floor into the tiny hallway. As she moved silently past the baby's room she noted that the sounds hadn't awakened her daughter either.

"Like father, like daughter," she snorted in envy to herself and walked into the smaller back room to peer out the open window.

The sound of the whimpering increased when she reached the window. By stretching up and squinting downward she could just see the rump of a Doberman puppy gyrating at a neighbor's gate. Still, there was no way to get a full view from upstairs. She decided to take a look from the downstairs windows.

The young woman padded back and forth. She ran from the cold slick tile of the kitchen to the warmth of the carpet in the dining room, trying to see enough to show her why the animal kept up that infernal whining.

The puppy seemed to be making sport with something held in its mouth. She saw him shaking whatever it was like a rubber toy. Yet the sounds the dog was making were full of fear and pain.

The woman surrendered to her need to understand and went outside for a better vantage point. Her line of vision from the porch was partially blocked by foliage and fences, but the air was singing with puppy screams.

Somehow the dog seemed to know the door had been opened. He stopped squirming and spotted her as soon as she saw him. His whines seemed to be directed straight to her. The appeal was overwhelming.

She dashed down the walkway, gazing across the fences, directly to the gate where the puppy lay. She saw that he was vainly jerking his head between the fence post and the gate. Somehow he had forced his head through the small opening and was trapped! Whatever he was shaking so vigorously was still hanging from his jaws.

His crying and writhing set her nerves jangling like the bells on a breeze-tossed windchime. The pitiful scene drew her out of her yard and around the alley; she caught herself just before she reached the gate under which the Doberman was trapped. She stood still. Her nearness to the dog seemed to ease him a little; his howling lessened to a steady moaning. Now she was able to discern that the puppy was shaking a can. It was firmly lodged between two of his upper teeth. Relief propelled her the last few steps to the gate. She knew she couldn't have stayed to help if he'd been gripping a bird or cat or even a rat!

She used her long nightgown as padding and knelt in front of the miserable little Doberman. The puppy's efforts to rid himself of the battered can had scraped a raw place on his silken snout and wedged it nearly up to his gum. Whining softly, the dog looked up and pulled his body toward her. That did it!

She was a short, wiry woman whose hands were small but strong. The limited space left for maneuvering made her size a distinct advantage. She could get as close to the ground as he without difficulty.

One slender arm reached through the opening. Her tiny hand rubbed his head and back for a little while. The other hand gently encircled his lower jaw. He did not resist. She grasped the offending can and slowly worked it backward and forward as she pulled it down. The dog lay absolutely still, even when her short fingers slipped into his mouth. She worked in slow motion - taking the utmost care. At last, the rim of the can slid off the edges of his pointed teeth. Only then did she release his jaw.

The dog's mouth stretched open. The woman leaned back, expecting a bark in her face. She was treated to a soft, high-pitched yet fearless sigh that made her laugh out loud. Her laughter ceased as abruptly as it had begun when she realized that her task was not yet completed.

She stretched both hands forward this time. Her supple fingers spread to enclose the skull, but she realized there was no room for his release that way. She closed her fingers and turned the dog's head trying to ease him back. He yelped in distress. She let go quickly.

Reaching inside again, she pushed the puppy back by putting pressure against his chest and shoulders. He protested mildly, and pulled forward again, laying his snout on her leg. The woman was so touched by this gesture of trust that she groaned in frustration. She stroked him absently as she tried to think of a solution to his dilemma.

She decided on a different tactic. She forced the dog onto his side, then pushed the elongated head slowly backward through the small opening. The plan was working! When his head was halfway free, the hinge on the gate jammed against the back of her hand. The pain made her forget to move slowly and she snatched her hand away. The hinge poked right into the dog's soft underjaw causing him to pull back to his original position in panic. He resisted all further efforts she made to turn him sideways after that. She was forced to think of some other way to free him.

She tried pulling the gate over to make the confining space wider. She tried to pick the lock on the chain which held the gate fast. She tried pushing the dog upwards, but he was too short to reach the larger space at the top and she wasn't strong enough to hoist him up to it. The cement path prevented her from freeing him underneath. Only the early hour caused her to discount the thought of screaming the dog's owner awake. Nothing was working in their favor.

Suddenly, the woman felt a chill. Her exertions and anxiety had made her body wet with sweat. The morning breezes cooled the cotton gown against her bare skin. She realized that she needed more clothing.

"Dog, you gonna cause me to catch a cold. I must be simple as you are, out here in my nightgown," crooned the young woman to the young dog. He responded by whining as though he understood her words.

She struggled up and brushed the dirt and hair from her hands. The Doberman began to squirm and cry out when she moved away. She turned back.

"Now be still. I'll be right back. Don't cry. I'm coming right back. Okay?"

The puppy yelped in confusion. Her desertion contrasted too much with the gentle tone of her voice. Then he lay still, watching her as long as he could. When she was out of his sight he seemed to listen and was silent until she disappeared into her kitchen.

The Doberman's Dilemma

His keening began the instant the lock clicked and it continued until he saw her running back toward him. A few minutes had passed while the young woman donned a robe and slippers and tied a scarf over her head. Then, she'd had to gather up a bottle of baby oil and smear shortening on a paper towel. She was upset and winded when she knelt down again.

"Will you please ... stop ... all that ... noise, ... dog? Didn't I tell you ... I was coming ... back? Now, you just ... shut up! I don't care 'bout you being mad .. I was cold! Besides, I needed to get this stuff to help us. So you just keep still and let me rub this oil on your dumb head. And don't you bite me either!"

Smiling at the dog and speaking in lullaby tones, the woman rubbed oil on both sides of the silken head. She had to alternate rubbing oil with stroking to keep the puppy calm. She smeared the shortening on the fence and gate posts and patted the dog. She rubbed more oil on the sleek head and patted the dog. She managed to smear oil over both hands by rubbing his head. Then she smiled into the dog's brown eyes and spoke.

"Well, if you can stand a little more pain, puppy, I think we've got it made. Okay, now I'm gonna push and you gotta pull. Go on; easy. Easy dog! Don't be in such a hurry. All right - good. You've got the idea now. Oh, thank goodness, its working! Now DON'T start crying and jerking your head, hear? Don't stop! You're almost free. Here. Let me get my hands out of your way. Hope you don't mind my hand pushing your nose! That's it, just ease on back. You're one smart dumb dog once you catch on, ain't cha?"

The young woman sat back on her haunches and watched as the young dog wriggled his lean black body back, back, then pulled his head free of the confining space.

The Doberman backed away from the gate on his belly. He looked at the woman's hands reaching for him and moved forward so she could rub his head. As she worked to clean off the excess oil and shortening with a towel, the puppy busied himself licking her hands. His rough tongue felt warm and ticklish enough to make her grin. She finished cleaning his head and withdrew her hands. Then a change in the dog's behavior caught her attention.

Just as she stood to leave, the dog slowly rose to his full height on stiffened legs. He stood stock still and stared right into her eyes. His head moved in a wide clockwise arc. His mouth opened and one friendly bark floated straight to the woman. She felt compelled to acknowledge his actions, so she nodded solemnly, saying, "You're welcome, pretty thing!" They exchanged looks of mutual joy.

Then it happened!

The dog lifted himself upward effortlessly. His body sailed sideways and soared through the air onto the grass. Leaping and prancing, he surrendered himself to pure, joyful exuberance. Ballet-like movements graced the dog's gyrations from ground to air and back again. He rolled and shimmied in the dew-laden green carpet; droplets flew all around him as he capered and thrust his body in every direction. Twisting and jumping, now on two legs, now on four, he circled and twirled in a majestic frenzy of freedom! Whines and yelps of relief and pleasure lent an almost musical quality to the happening.

The woman stood transfixed. She watched and listened to the ecstatic animal in awe. The depth of the dog's emotions affected her deeply. What she saw unfolding before her was the ultimate reward for her efforts.

Every move the dog made bespoke utter happiness for both of them. He felt it and celebrated. She felt it and smiled through her tears. His release and her relief bound them. She watched him for a long time – motionless, yet delighted. She would have applauded if she hadn't been spellbound!

Later, when the young woman reluctantly moved away, the puppy went right on celebrating his freedom.

When she reached her porch, she looked over at the young dog. He slowed his movements, lifted his head to send her one more friendly bark and promptly returned to his playful prancing. She laughed in amazement, rejoicing with him one last time before she closed the kitchen door.

During the day, the young husband heard the whole story from beginning to end. He chided his "foolish" wife, "You mean you actually went out of here in your nightgown? I just hope you haven't caught pneumonia! Do you have any idea what could have happened to you? Out there in that alley all by yourself that time in the morning! Why couldn't you just mind your own business? I never know what you're going to do next." He was forced to pause for a deep breath and then, giving his wife a suspicious look, he asked, "What are you thinking about now?"

She responded to him with a faraway look and said softly, "Did you know a dog could dance?"

Storytelling

Storytelling

Families told the first tales thousands of years ago, and still do.

Storytelling has probably been around as long as people walked the earth. Storytelling is the root of literature, theatre, opera, and even newspapers.

Storytelling is found in all cultures. It involves the story, the storyteller and the listener. It is a shared experience of emotions, wonder and magic.

Who told the first stories?

No one knows. But a tale about brothers was discovered in an ancient Egyptian manuscript. The story is more than 3,000 years old and is believed to be the oldest story in written form.

But storytelling is older than writing. The first stories were told by families sitting around a campfire. As the families grew into clans and began to spread out and travel, the stories traveled with them. The families passed these stories from generation to generation. We call these stories folktales.

During the ages, the art of oral storytelling was kept alive by troubadours, balladeers, and minstrels of Europe. Griots (GREE-ohs) - singing storytellers who preserved family histories and legends - and priests, monks, and philosophers of China, India and Persia.

Collections of stories have been gathered by anthropologists, folklorists, and missionaries.

There are different types of stories: myths, fables, fairy tales, "how and why" stories and stories about legends and heroes. It is important to remember that styles of stories can overlap. A fable can have elements of the how-and-why style; a fairy tale can have elements of a fable.

A folktale from West Africa says, "All stories belong to Anansi (Ah-non-see)." Anansi is the magic Spider Man. He weaved a web up to the Sky God and received the box of stories. Anansi brought them to Earth and gave them to everyone.

Today, there is a rebirth of storytelling by professional storytellers. These tellers are known for their unique style and the stories they tell. They have made storytelling a comtemporary art form and a career as well. Their message is to keep storytelling alive and fresh. Hopefully, families will continue to preserve the tradition in their homes.

In this country, the public library and the school systems have used storytelling to promote reading.

Stories come from our dreams, ancestors, surroundings, personal experiences, and most importantly, our imagination.

The imagination is the key that unlocks the world of storytelling. In your imagination you can see anything, be anything, and do anything.

As the saying goes, "I give the story to you. Take what you like and pass it on down to others."

© 1984 Linda Goss, The Traveling Storyteller

How I Make A Story A Part Of Myself

1. Block out an area of interest and/or read widely until one story "grabs" you.
2. Duplicate (if story is written) or write it in your own words.
3. Saturate yourself with this story. Read it over and over.
4. Block it. (A term used in directing plays)

Example: Story - MOSEOATUNYA OR THE SMOKE THAT THUNDERS *
LEARN BEGINNING SENTENCE

> The river
> Zaweisi
> Family, how they felt about courage
> Konkela's story
> Zaweisi's story
> Konkela's wife, her plea
> Zaweisi's answer
> The wife leaves her gift
> The wife's farewell and sacrifice of herself
> What happened to Zaweisi

LEARN ENDING SENTENCE – Place this in outline form on file card.

5. Rehearse, using the card, to yourself as you go through the day.
6. Practice to family, friends and/or tape.
7. Pray Psalm 19:14, Philippians 4:13.
8. Forget yourself as much as you can, and let the story come "through" you, the medium.

NOTES

At first glance this may seem an enormous task. But it is worth the effort. I find when I have done this, the story NEVER leaves me. Even after years have passed I can pick up the file card and the story comes back. I use the term "learn" or "possess" rather than memorizing. I do not worry about exact words. It is ideas, concepts, scenes that are like a skeleton that you clothe with words. I learn in depth four or five stories a year. Other stories you may choose to talk about, giving what is needed to relate, with excerpts that you learn.

YOU **ARE** A STORYTELLER! May God bless your gift. Love, John 13:35

Mary Carter Smith
© 1981

*From Mary Carter Smith's tape, **Stories and Songs**

Tidbits For Telling Stories

Choosing a Story

Does the story appeal to you? In a quick reading or listening does it capture your attention and involve you in what is happening? (Does it "grab" you?) You **MUST** like it to expect others to like it.

Are the characters interesting, believable, and fun to work with? Are there enough contrasts among them for you to portray them or at least give suggestions of differing characteristics? It is wise to keep the major characters to a few in number.

Select a story filled with action – with one suspenseful event building on another to the climax.

Have an arresting introduction.

Be aware of sensory images as, "Her skin was like black velvet."

Be aware of the length of a story. Beginning storytellers may try to keep stories within five to seven minute range. Some may be shorter. Ten minutes may be long enough to tell a short story; the folktales may be shorter. As you gain in experience you will get a "feel" for length, by the reaction of your listeners. **Telling time** and **reading time** are not the same.

Be aware of telling the appropriate story for your audience.

Decide whether to use first or third person in the telling.

You may decide to change setting and nationality of characters.

You may adapt a story by deleting plot incidents, minor characters and description.

Using Dialogue, rather than constant "and the man said," "the queen answered," etc.

Focus your attention on **TWO THINGS:**

1. The story (see it and feel it happen **NOW**)
2. Your listeners (let them know you care about them)

Facing Stage Fright

1. There is no "pat" cure.
2. Gain experience
3. Be prepared
4. "Sense" the audience and react to it
5. I repeat Philippians 4:13:
   "I can do all things through Christ, which strengtheneth me."

Costuming

Use to highlight and personalize your sessions if you are comfortable doing so.

Pitfalls

AVOID:

Standing perfectly immobile

Having too many gestures

Ignoring disruptive behaviour

Using some ethnic language with some groups that find it objectionable

Looking **DRAB**

Seeming insecure/scared

Having a monotonous voice

Having your story **too long.**
When you see you're losing interest, cut/change/stop.

Pacing back and forth

Mary Carter Smith
© 1981

*To Faye
Here's good cooking
to a find woman
and wonderful person —
all the best —
all the time
[signature]*

The Griots' Cookbook

GRIOT: (Say gree-oh)
A word from French West Africa meaning, among other things, a storyteller.

"In Africa the griots sang the songs, wrote and recited the poetry, remembered the history, told the stories and passed on whatever was worthwhile to everyone in the community."

Mary Carter Smith
Official Griot of Baltimore City